I0476184

# OCEAN

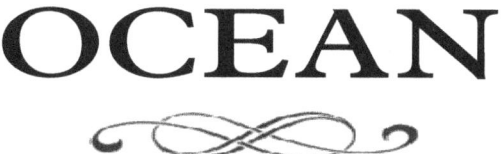

## Adult Coloring Book

- 36 Whimsical Ocean Designs
- Beginner to Experienced Level Patterns
- Hours of Stress Relief and Relaxation
- Single Sided Pages to Prevent Bleed Through
- Perfect Size for Framing
- Great Gift for Sea Lovers

*Color. Relax. Enjoy.*

Printed in the United States of America

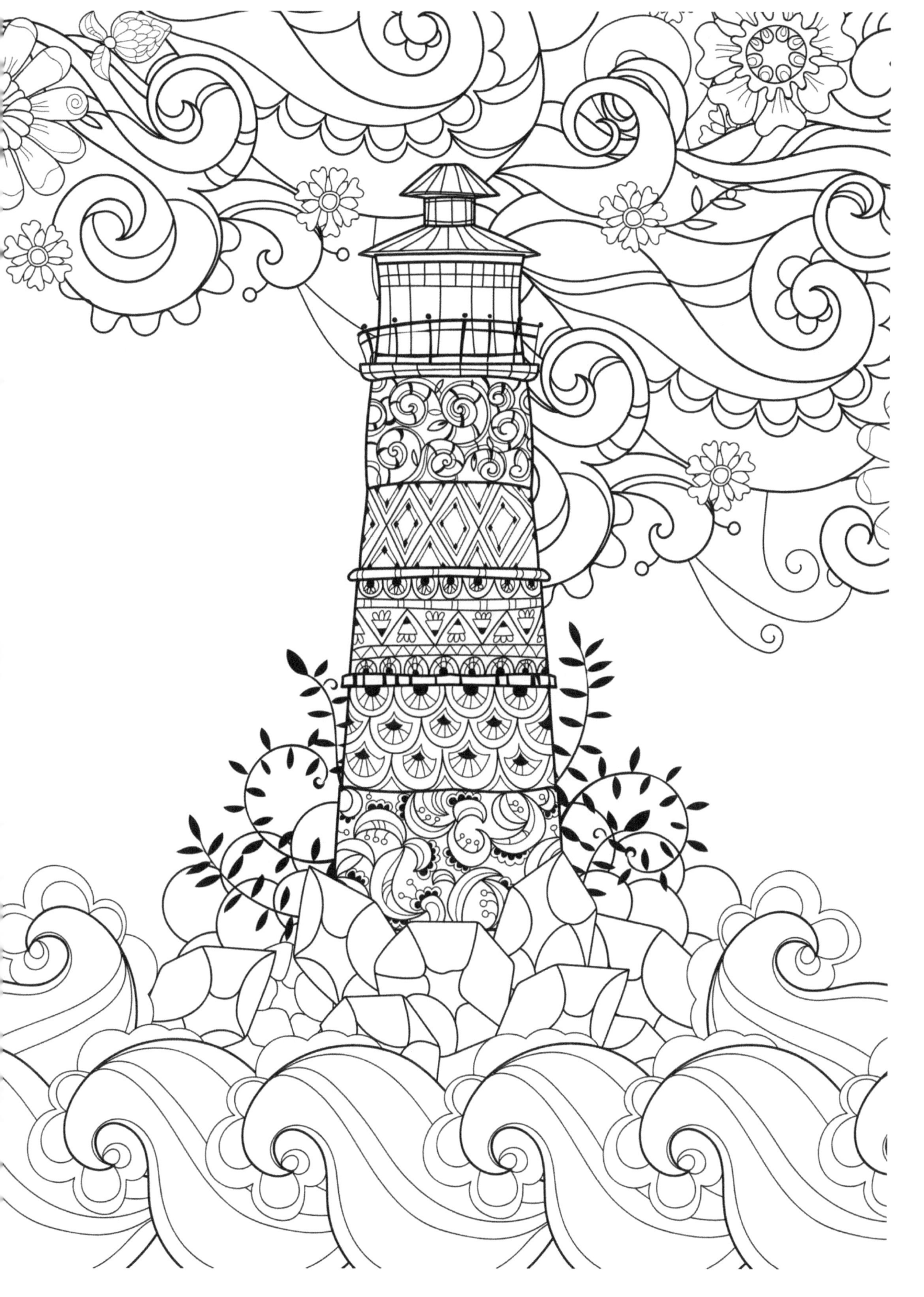

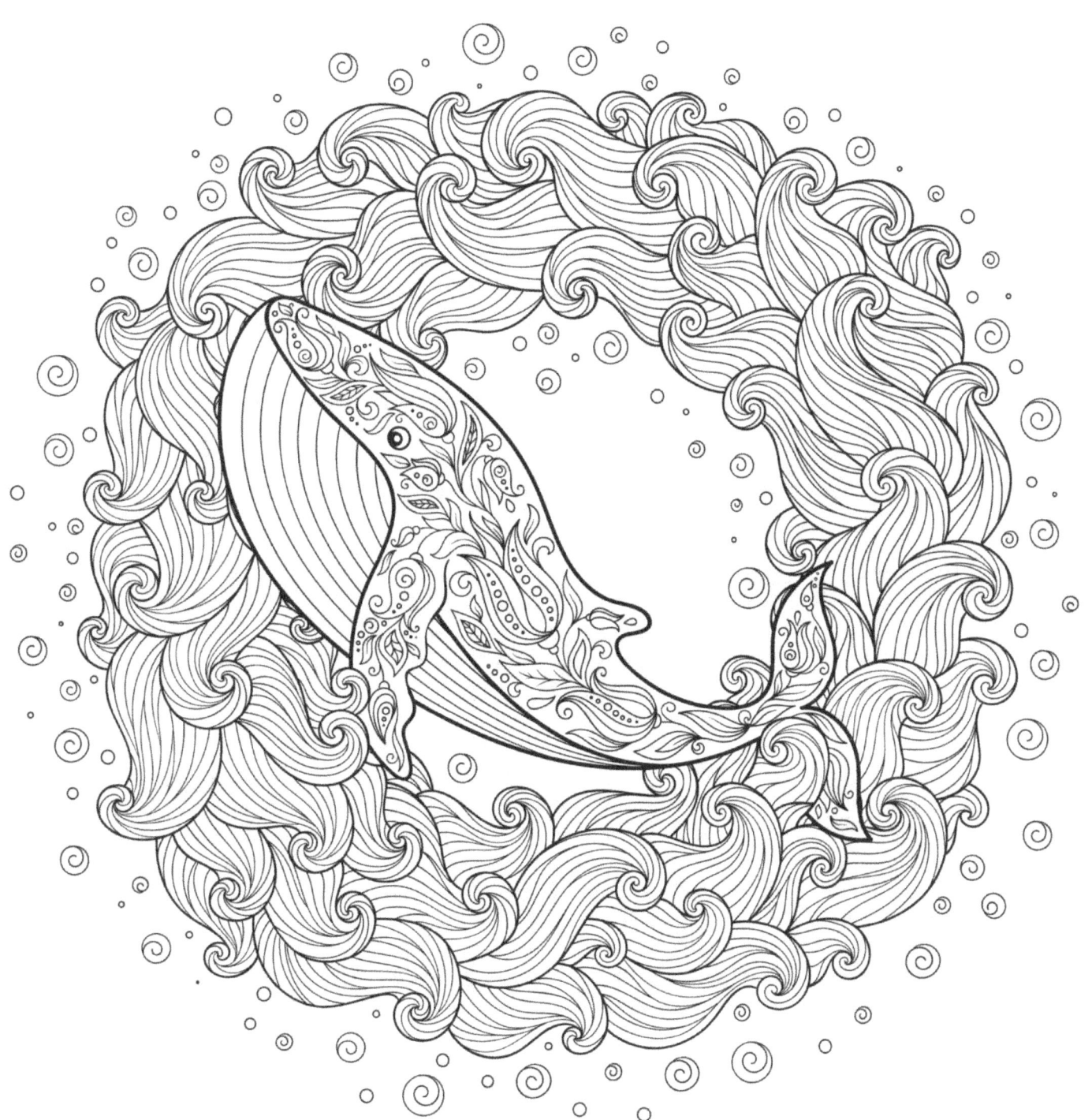

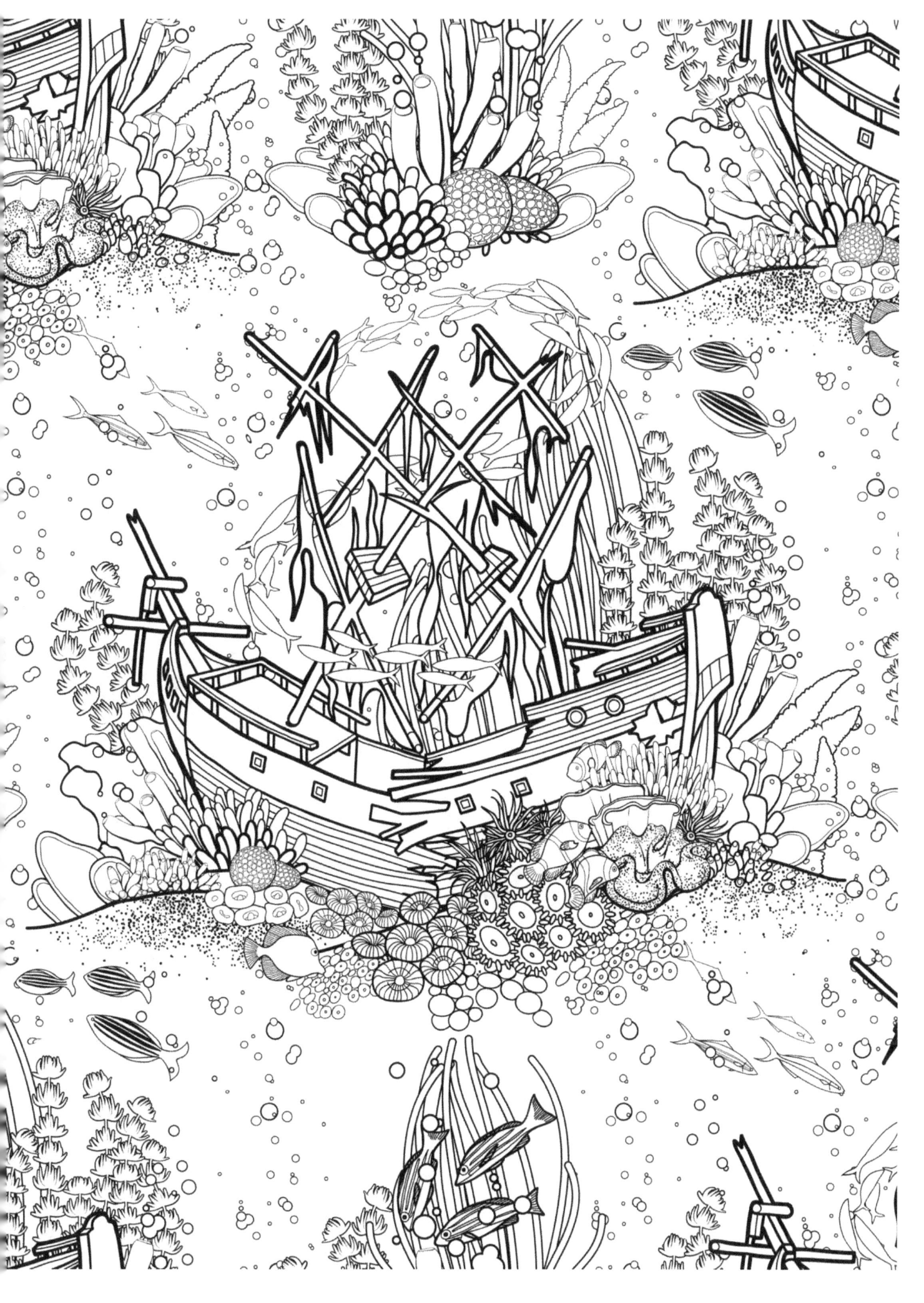

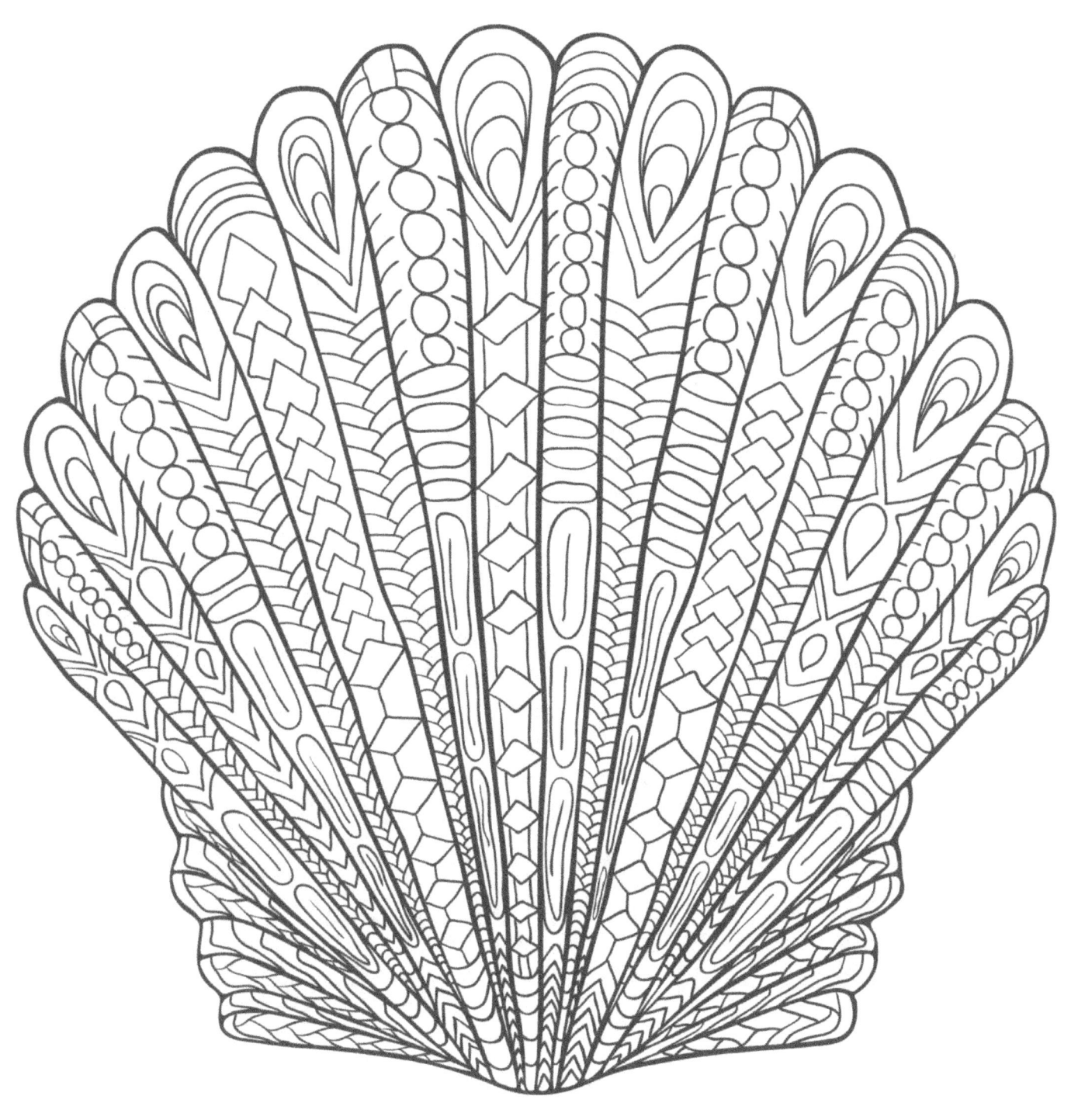

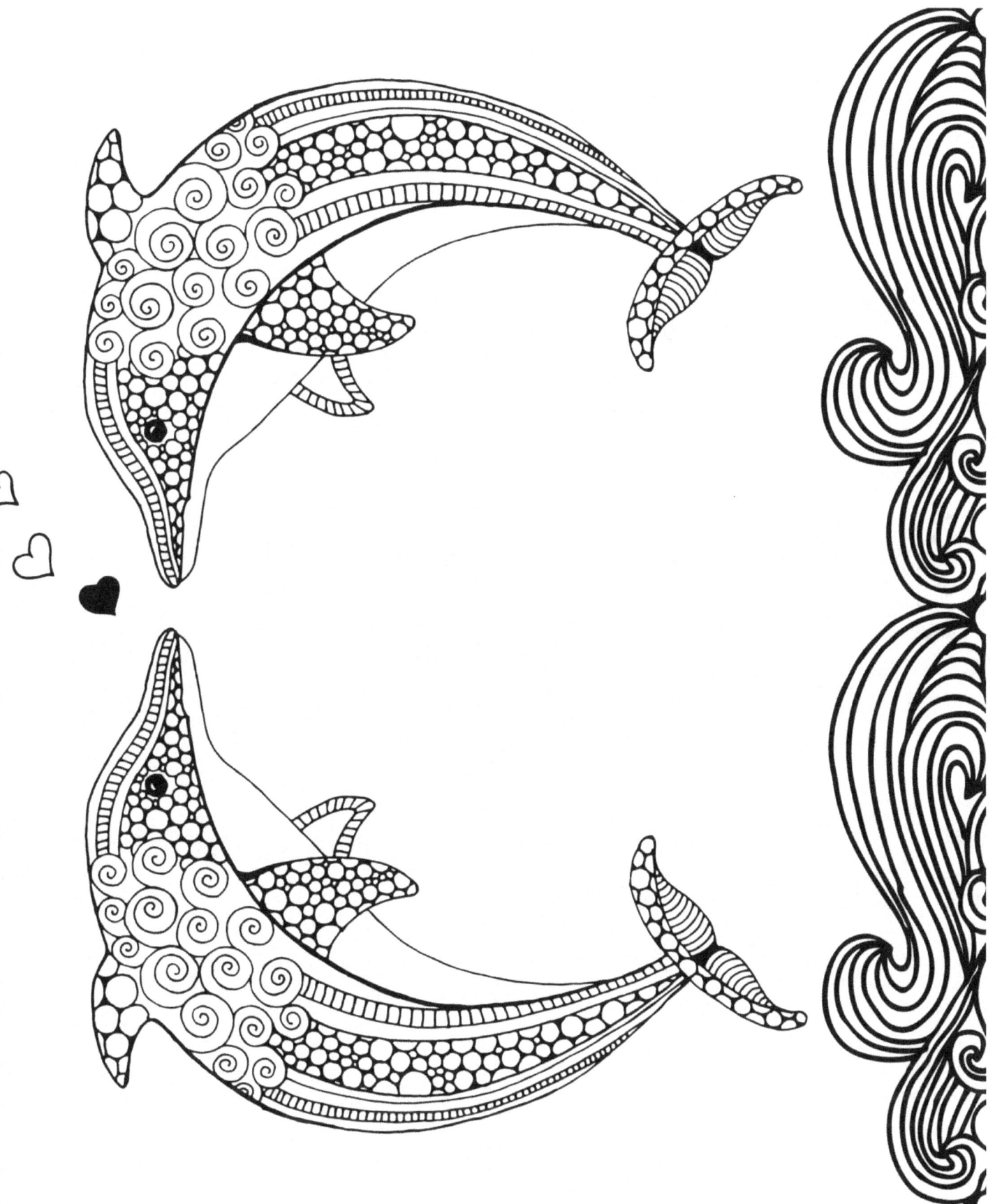

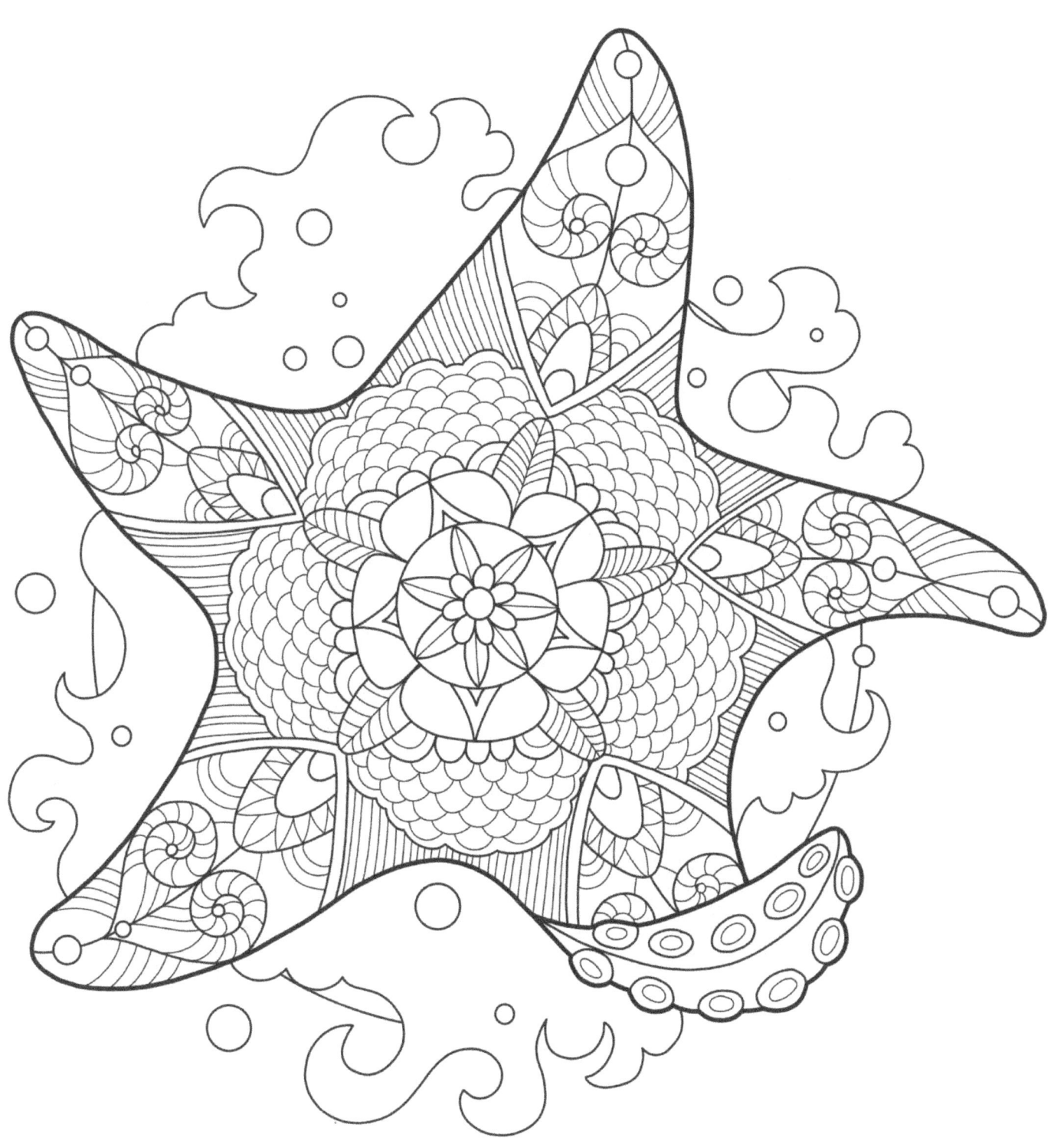

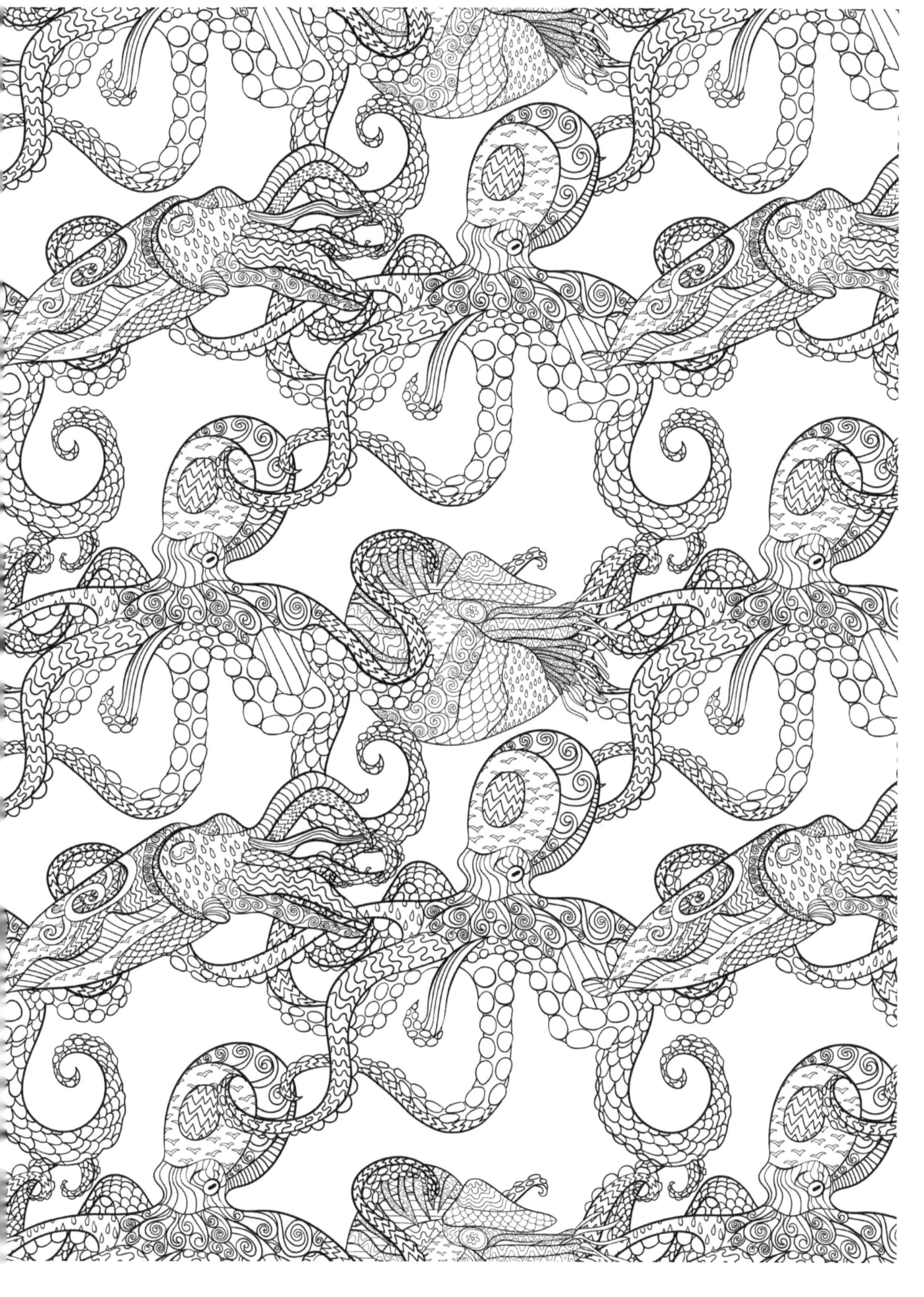

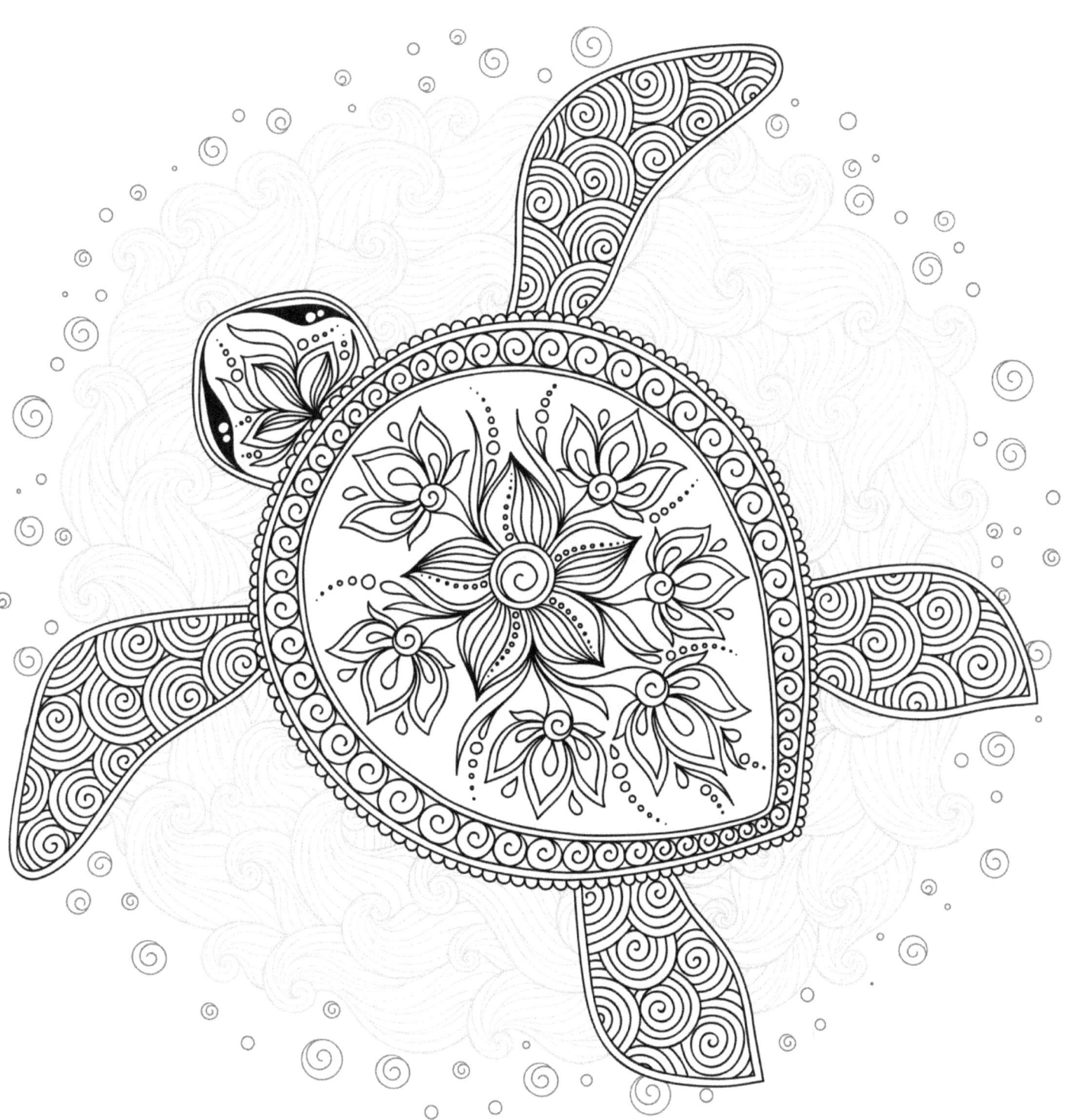

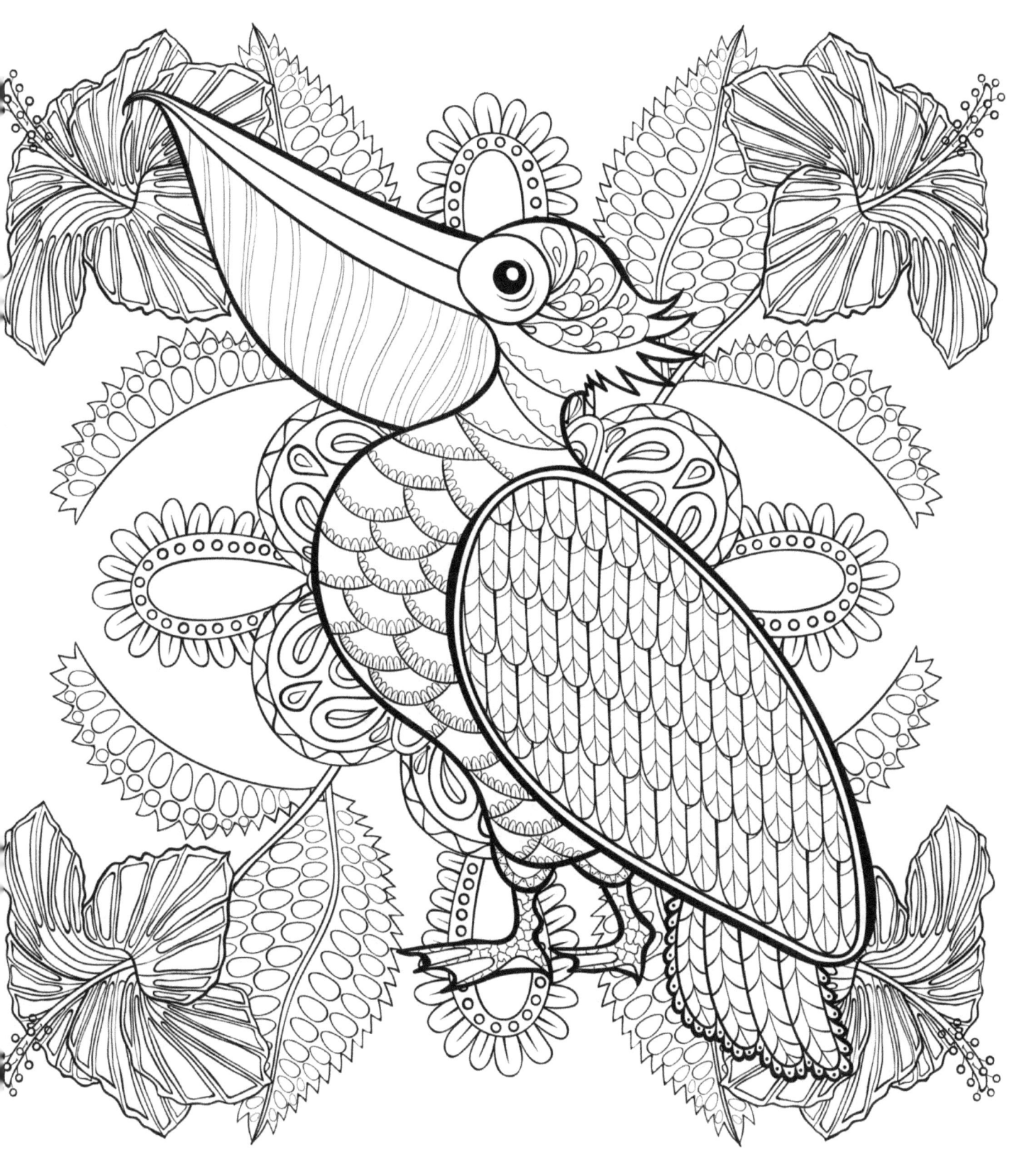

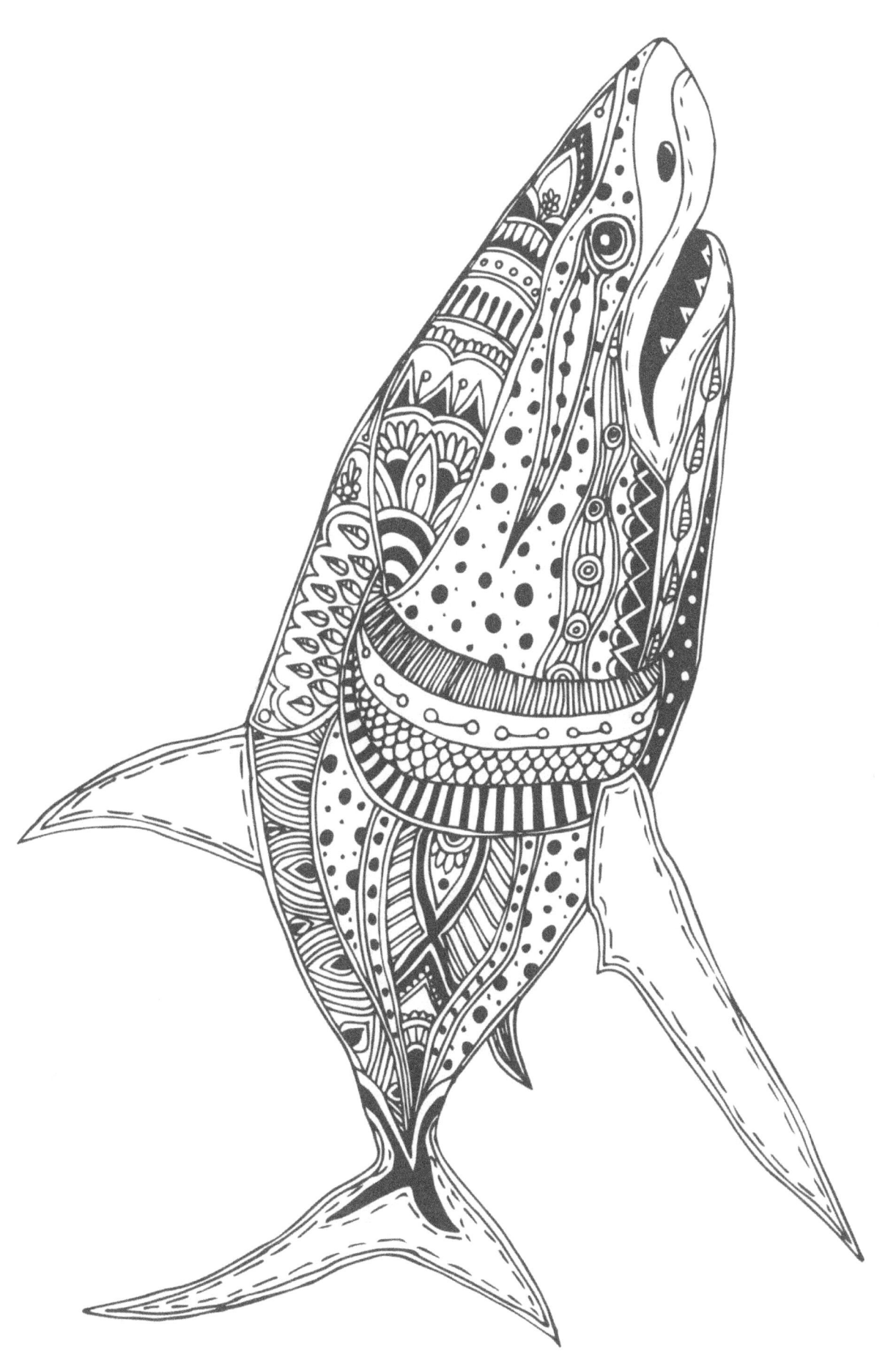

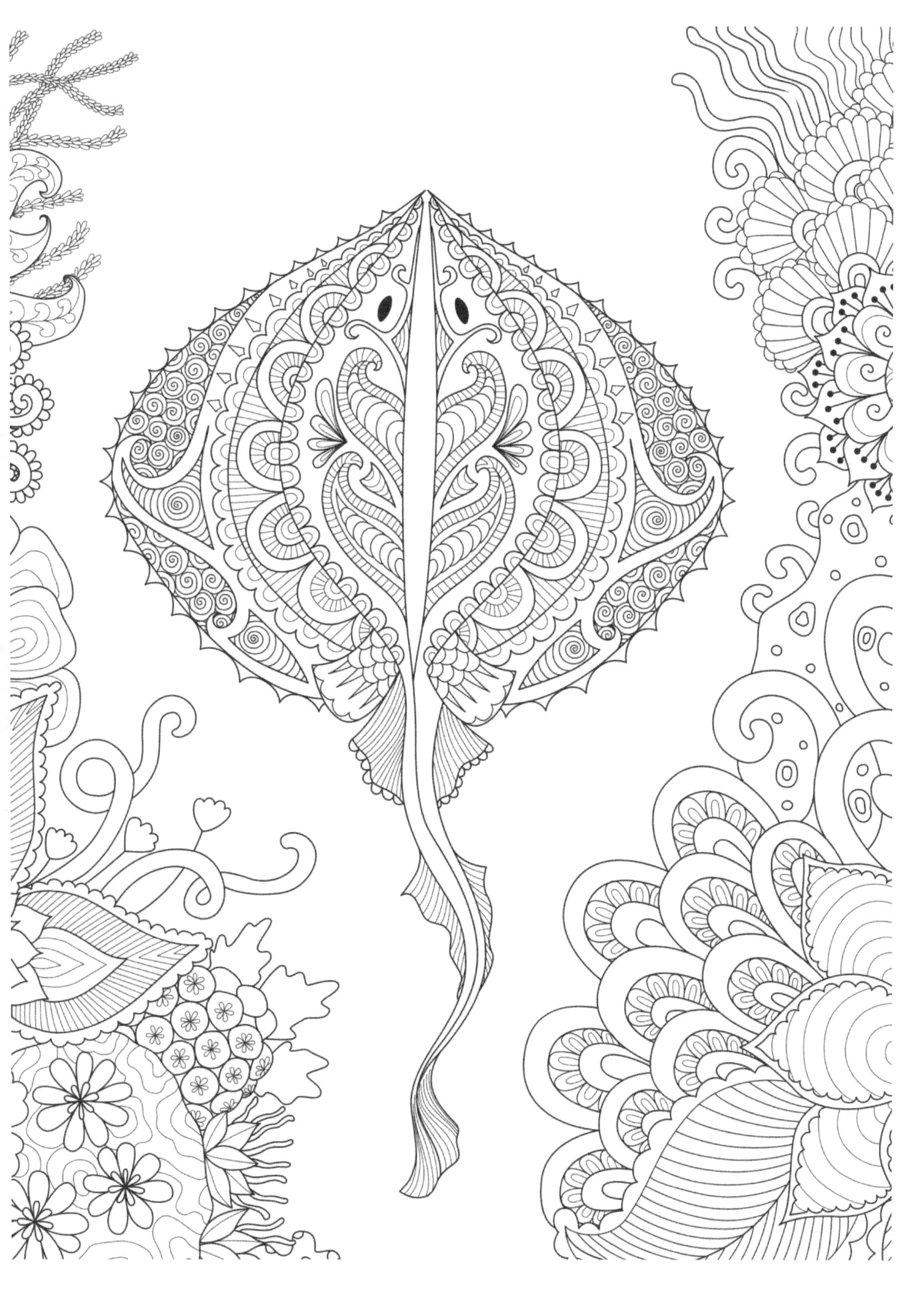

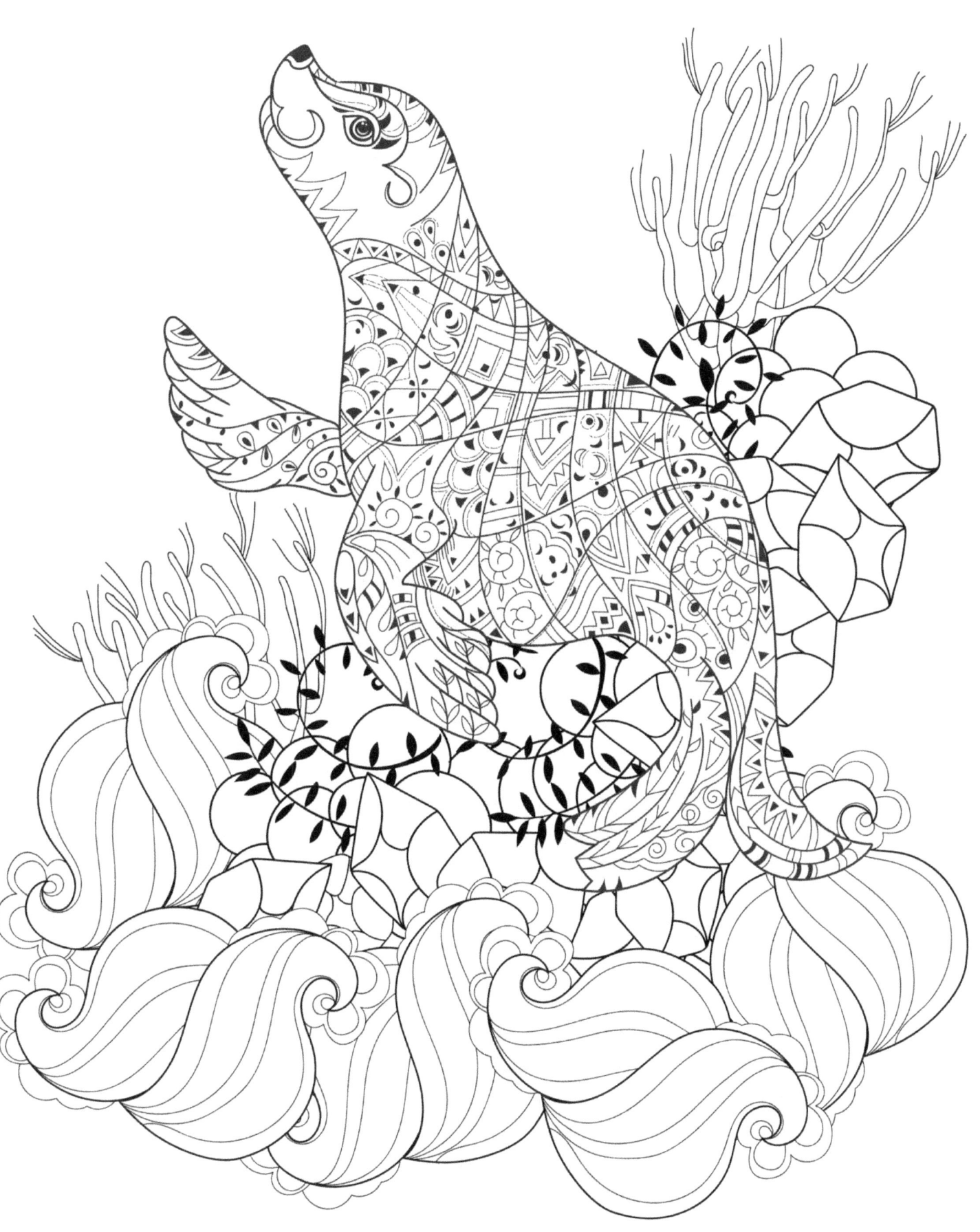

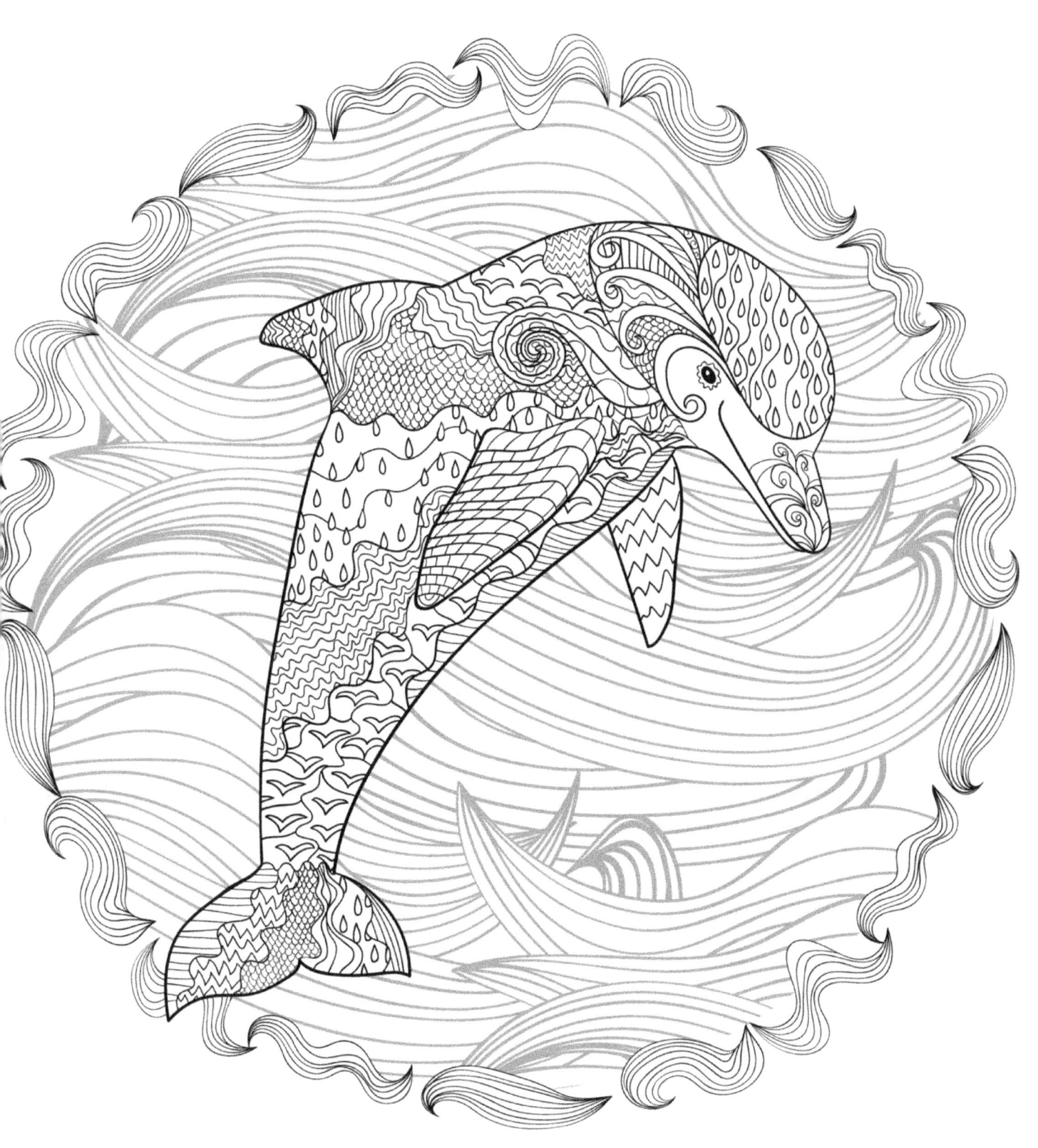

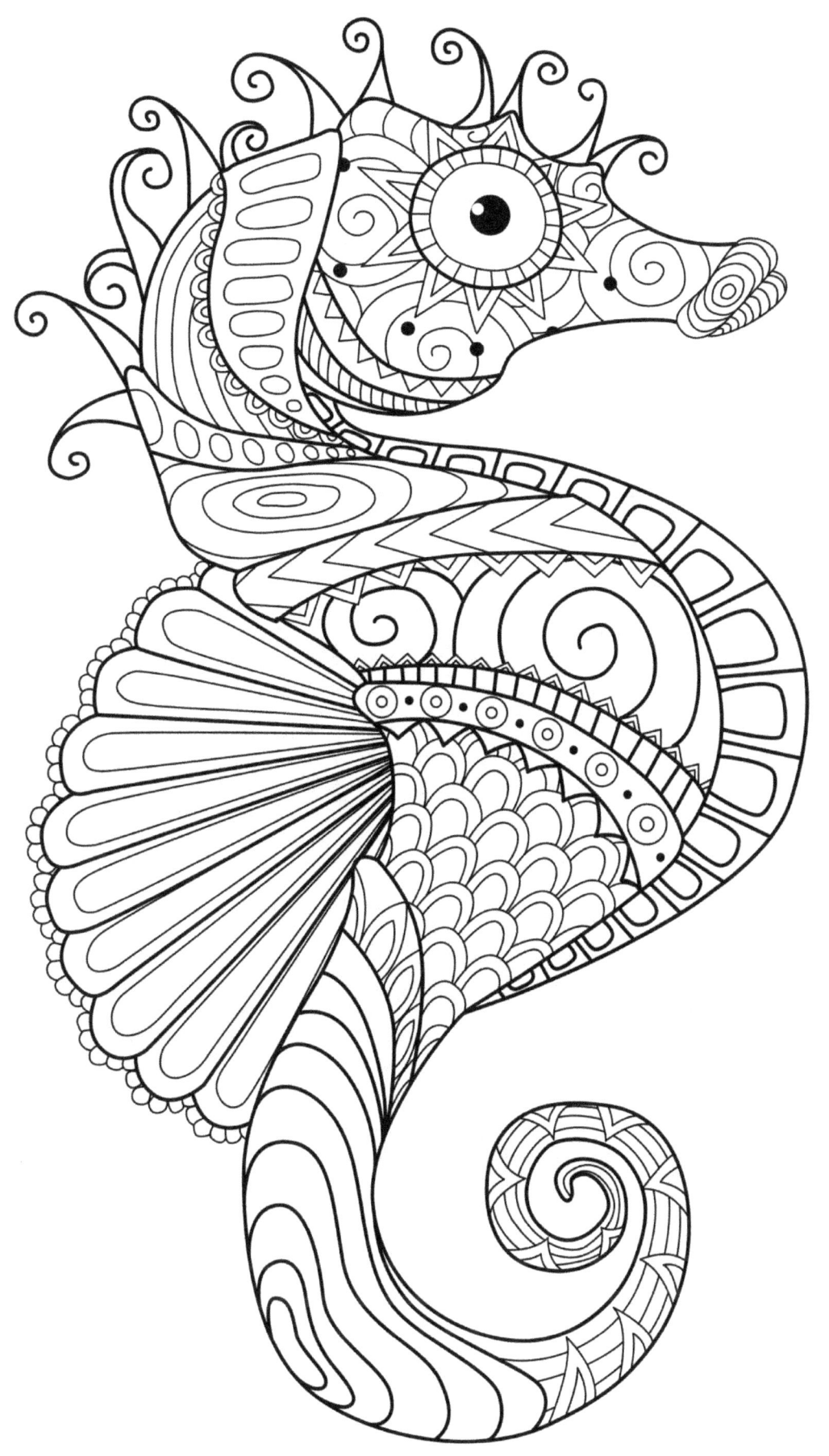

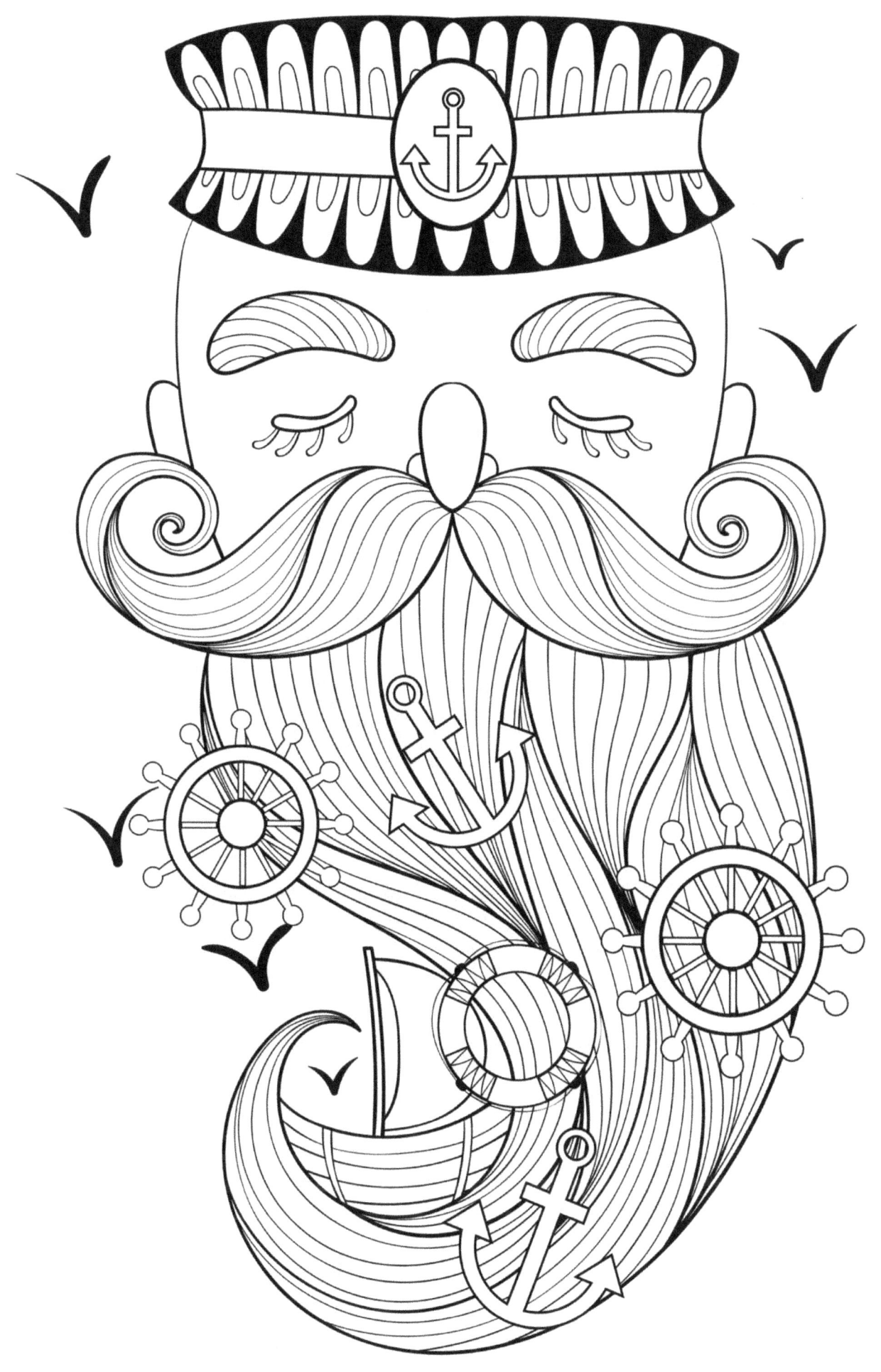

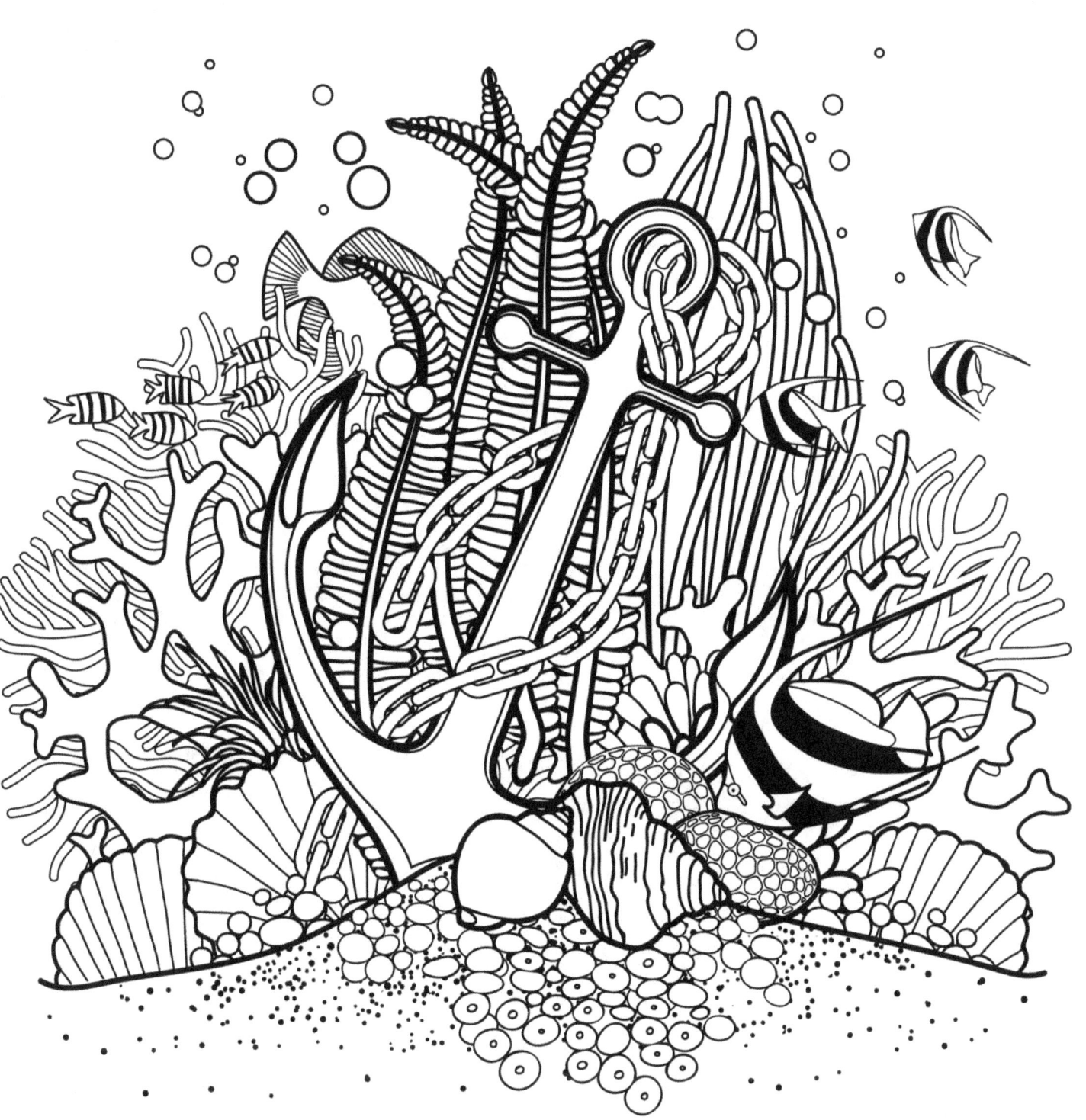

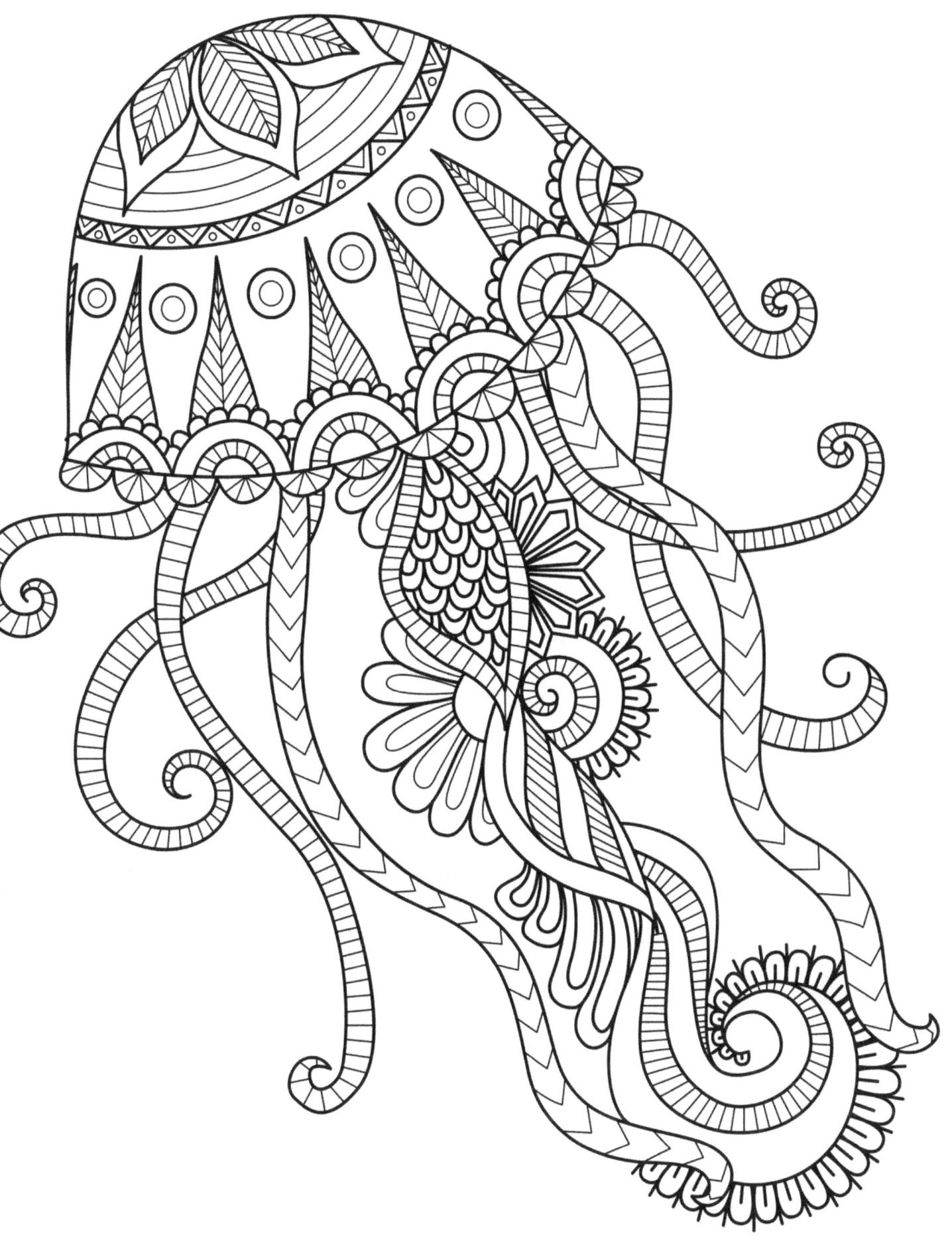

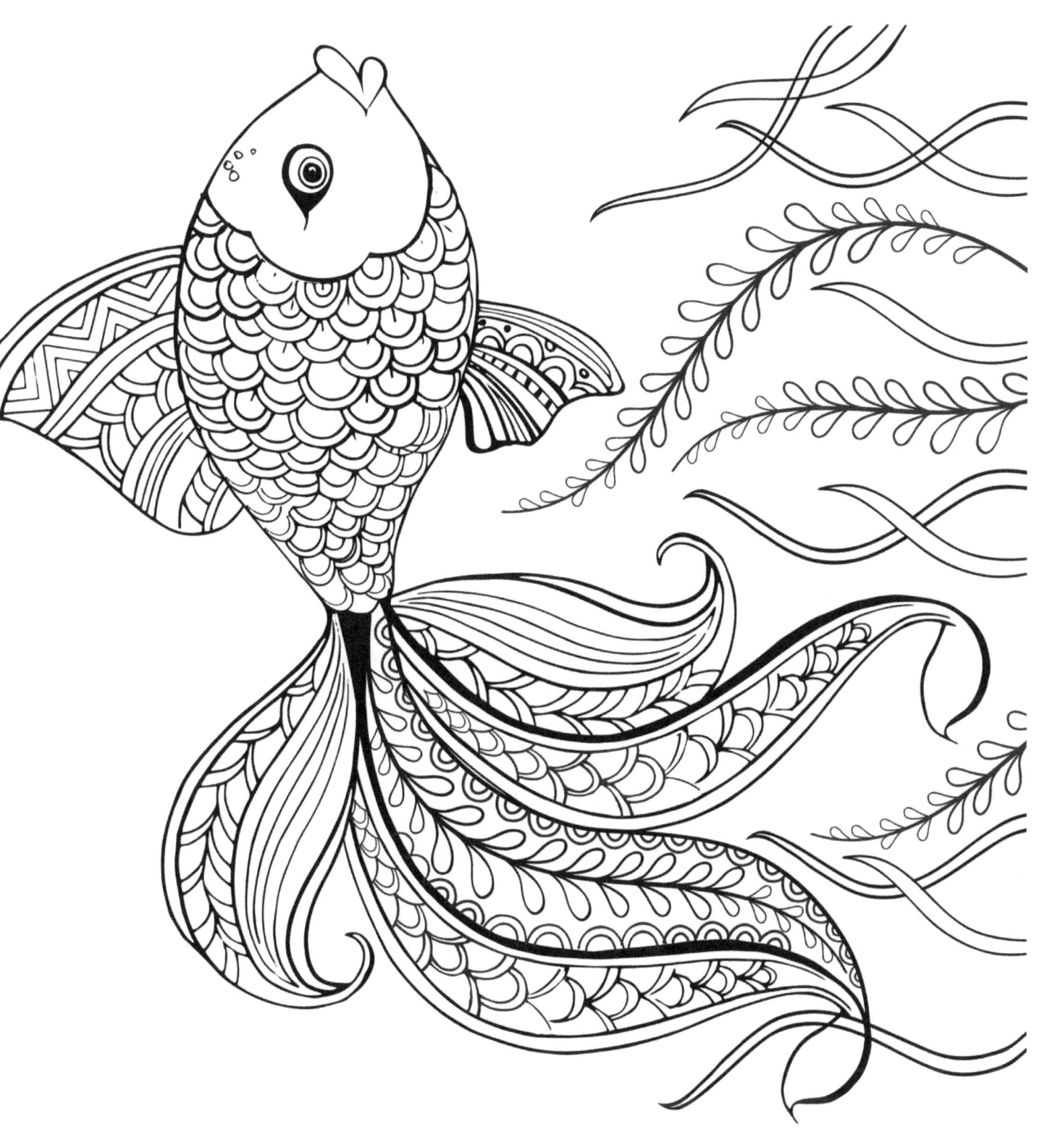

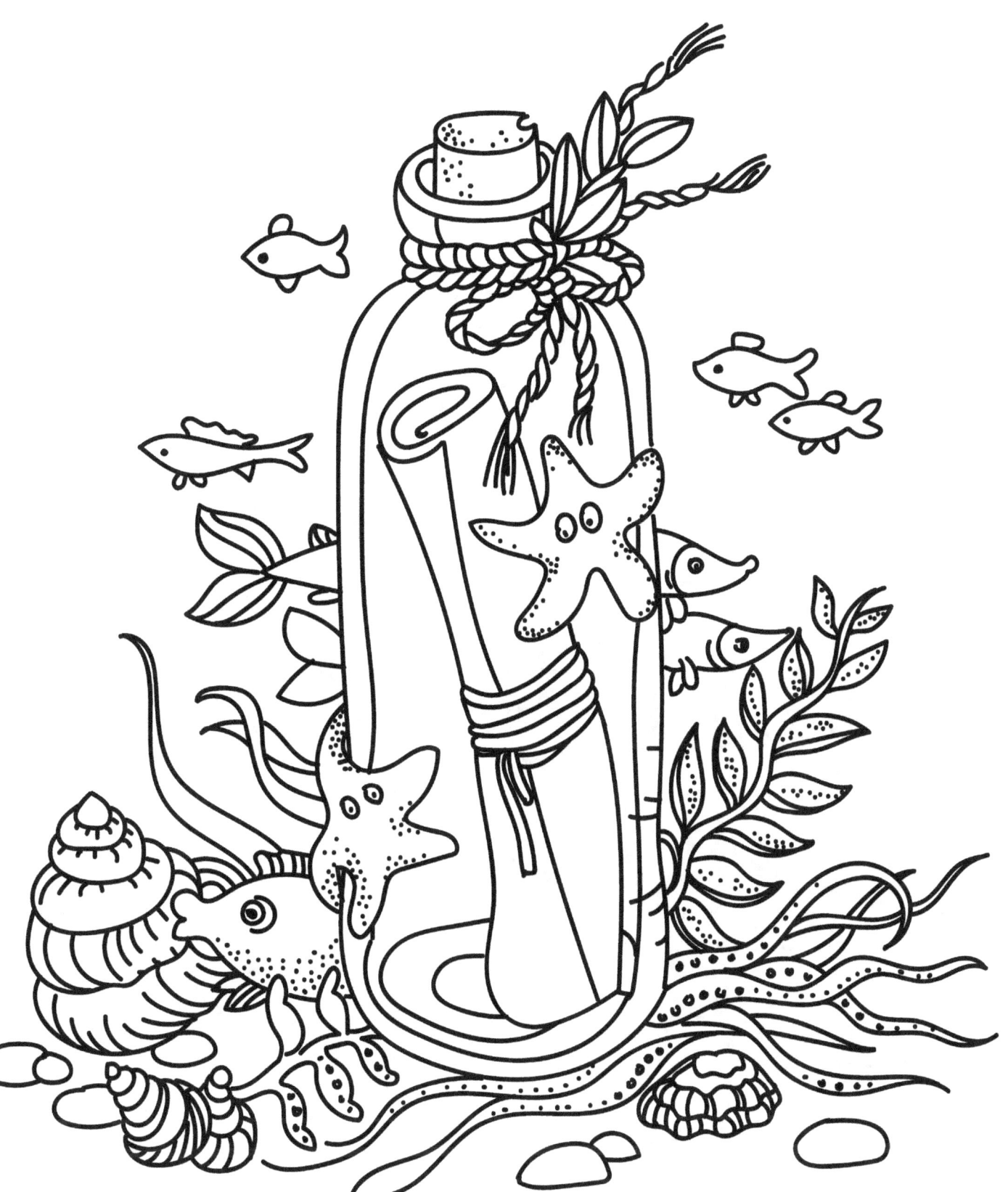

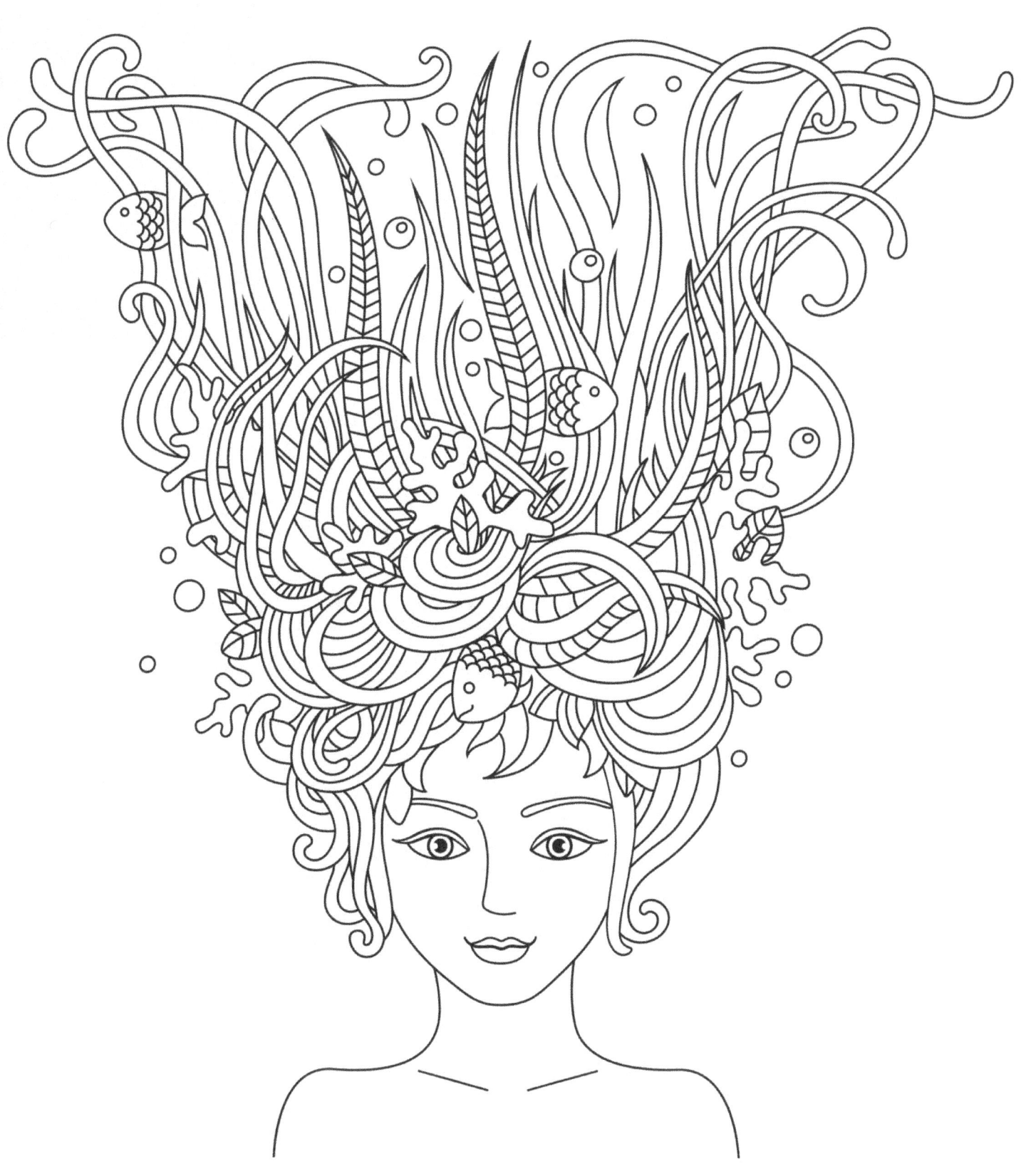

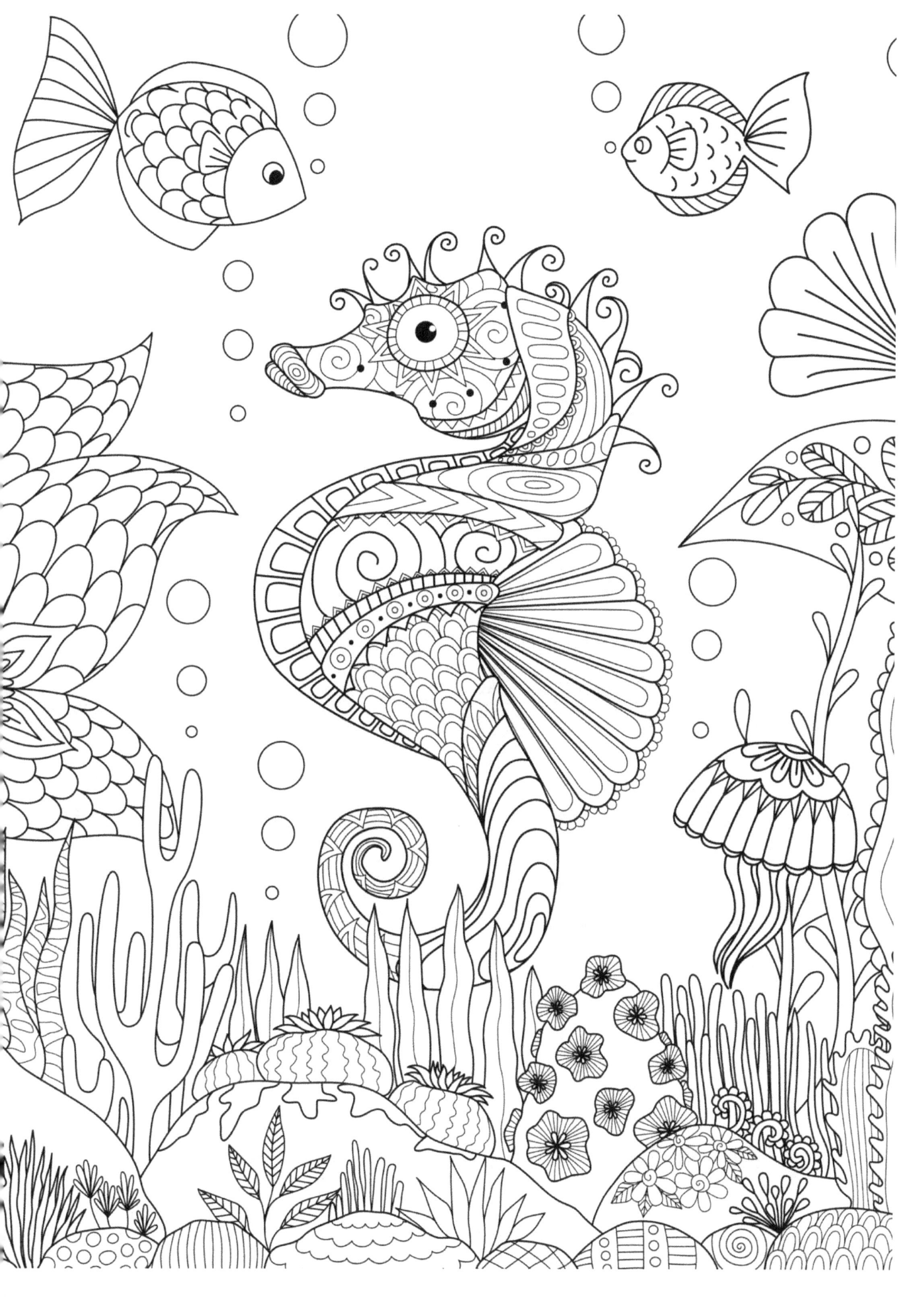

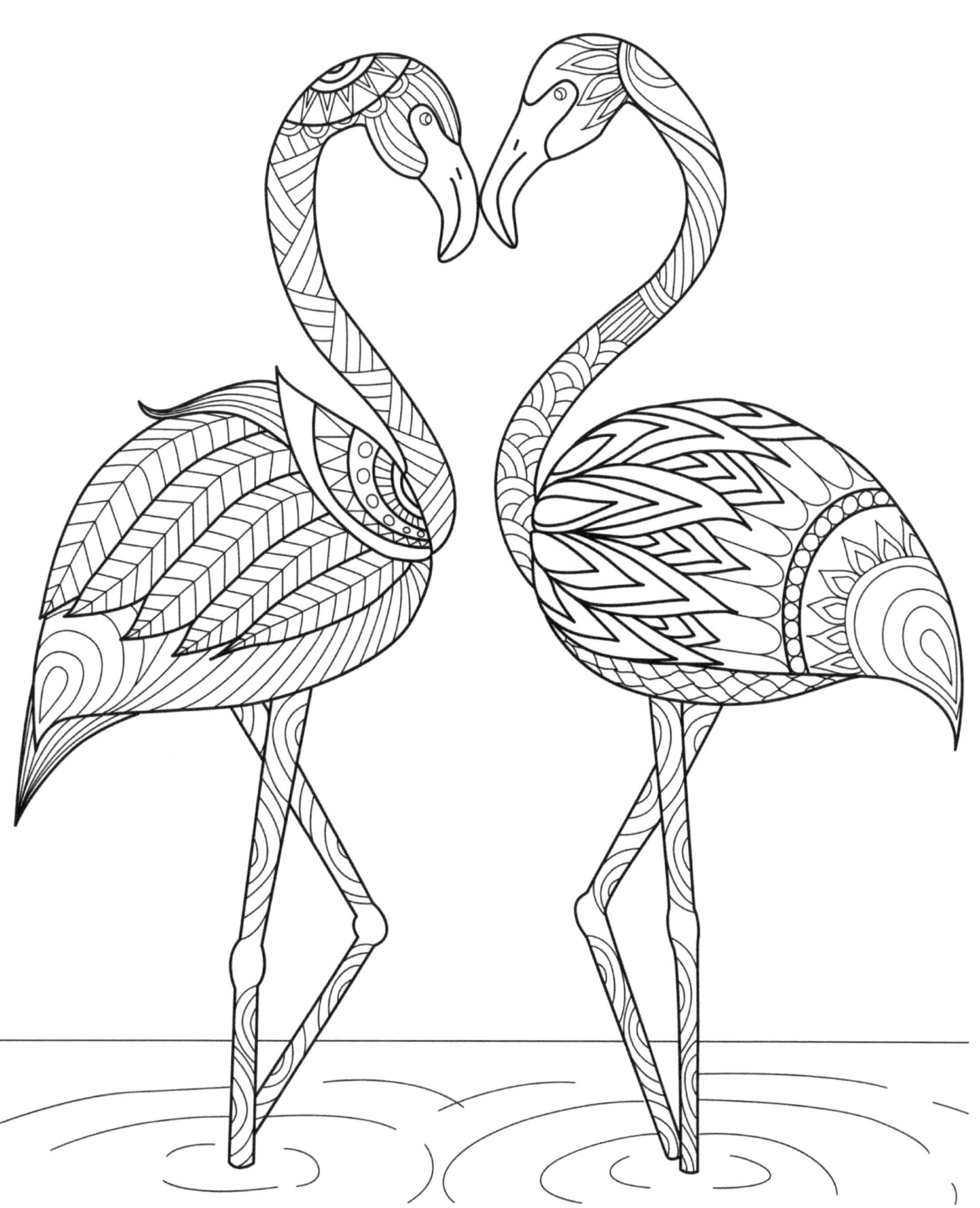

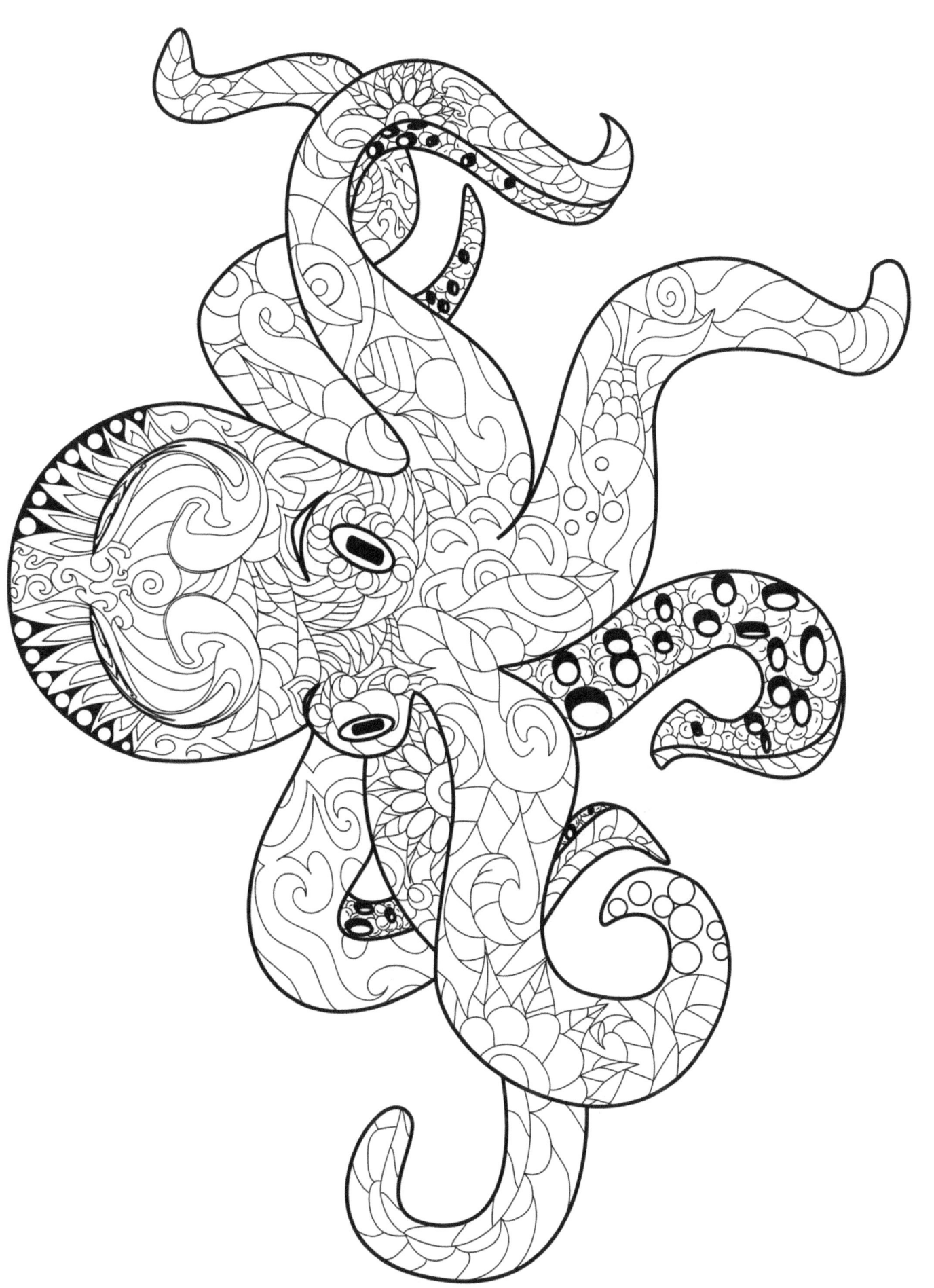

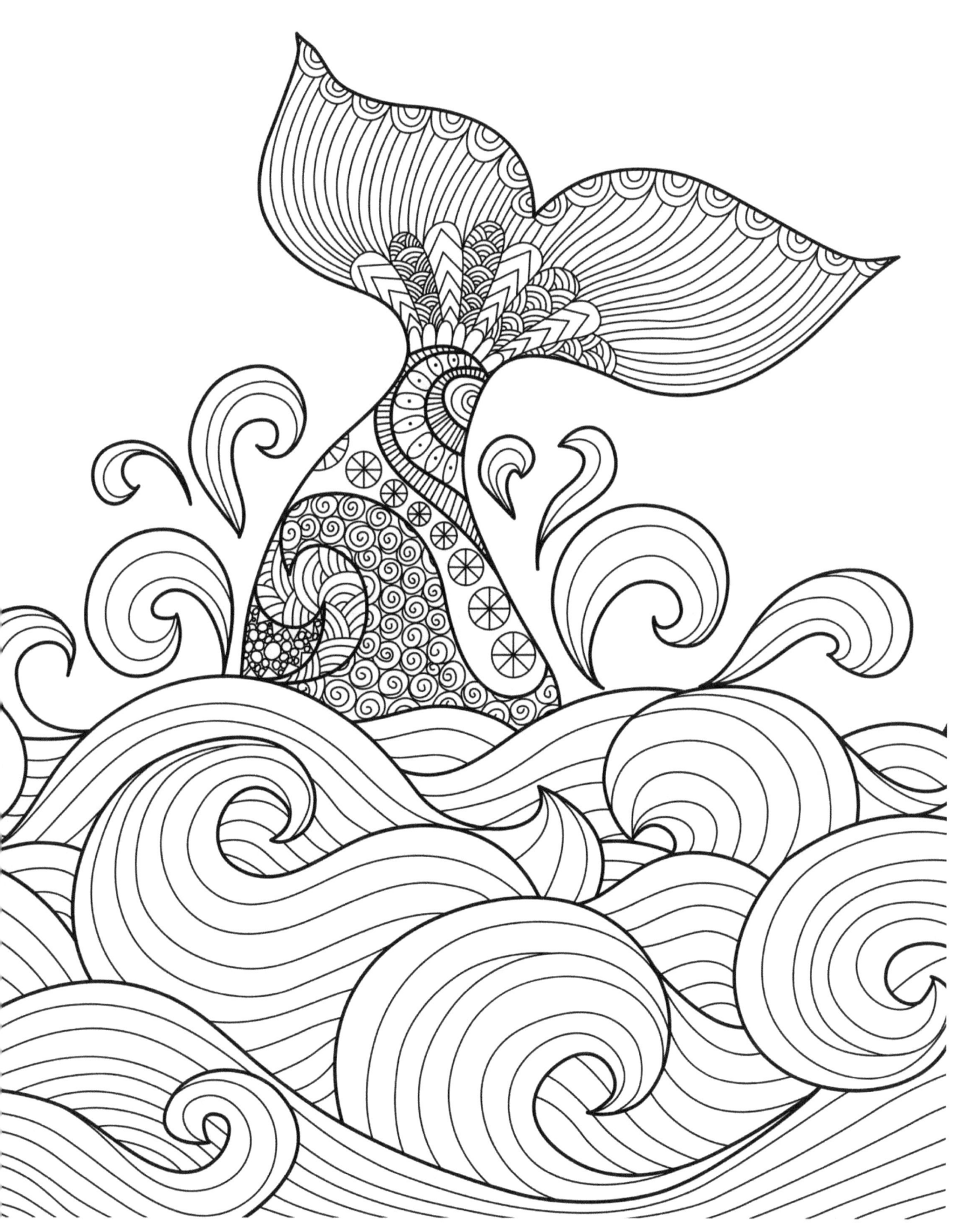

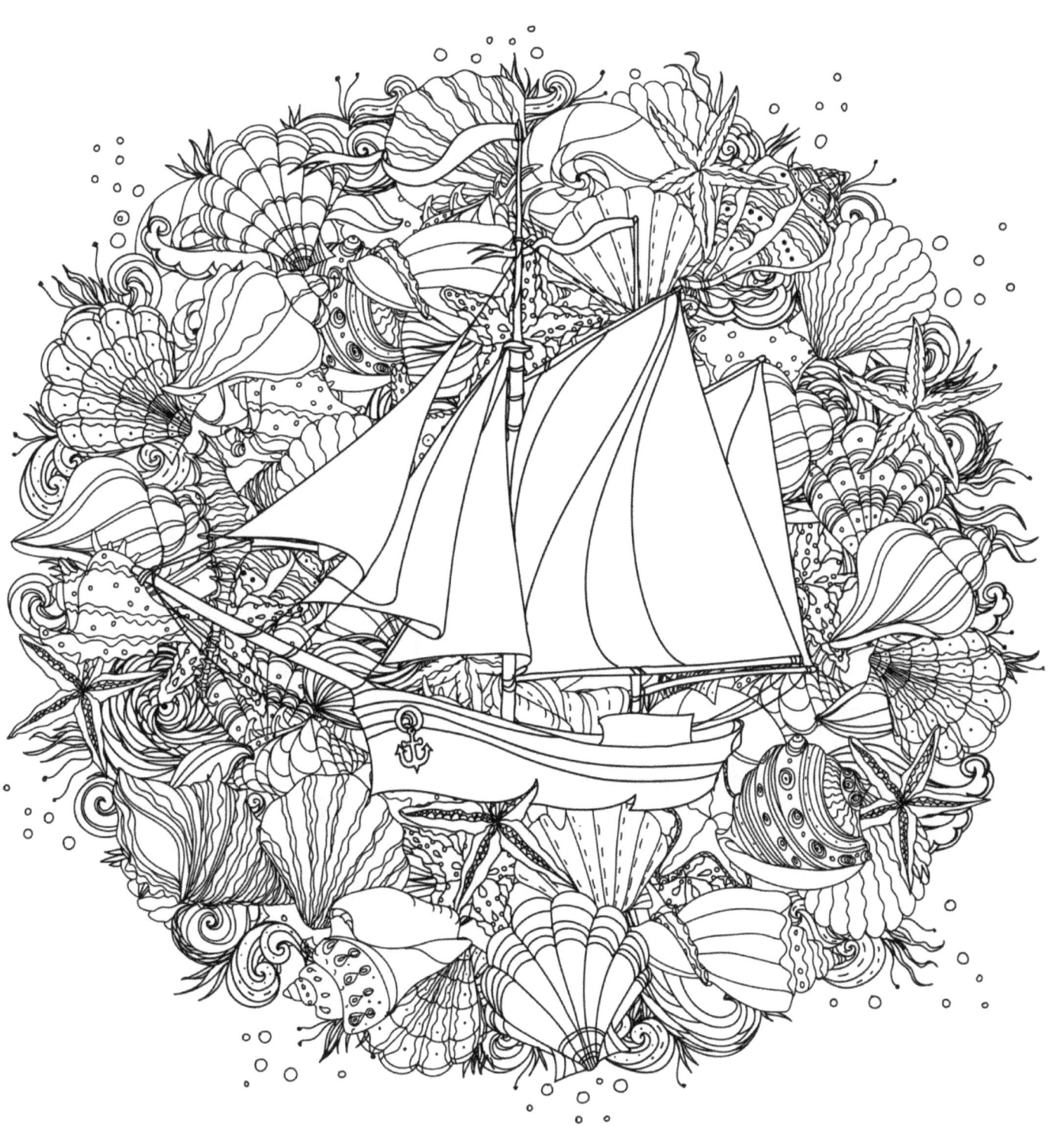

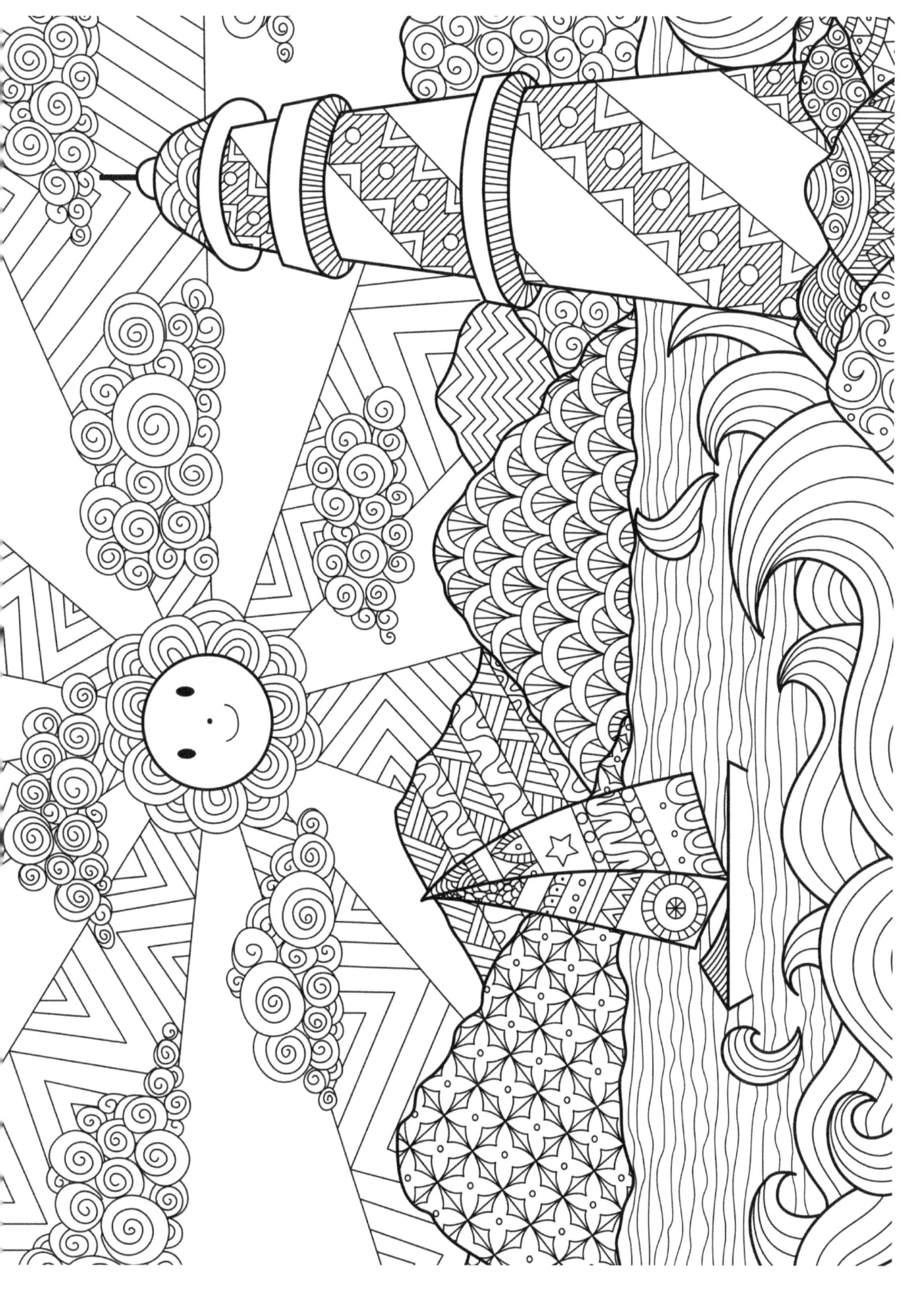

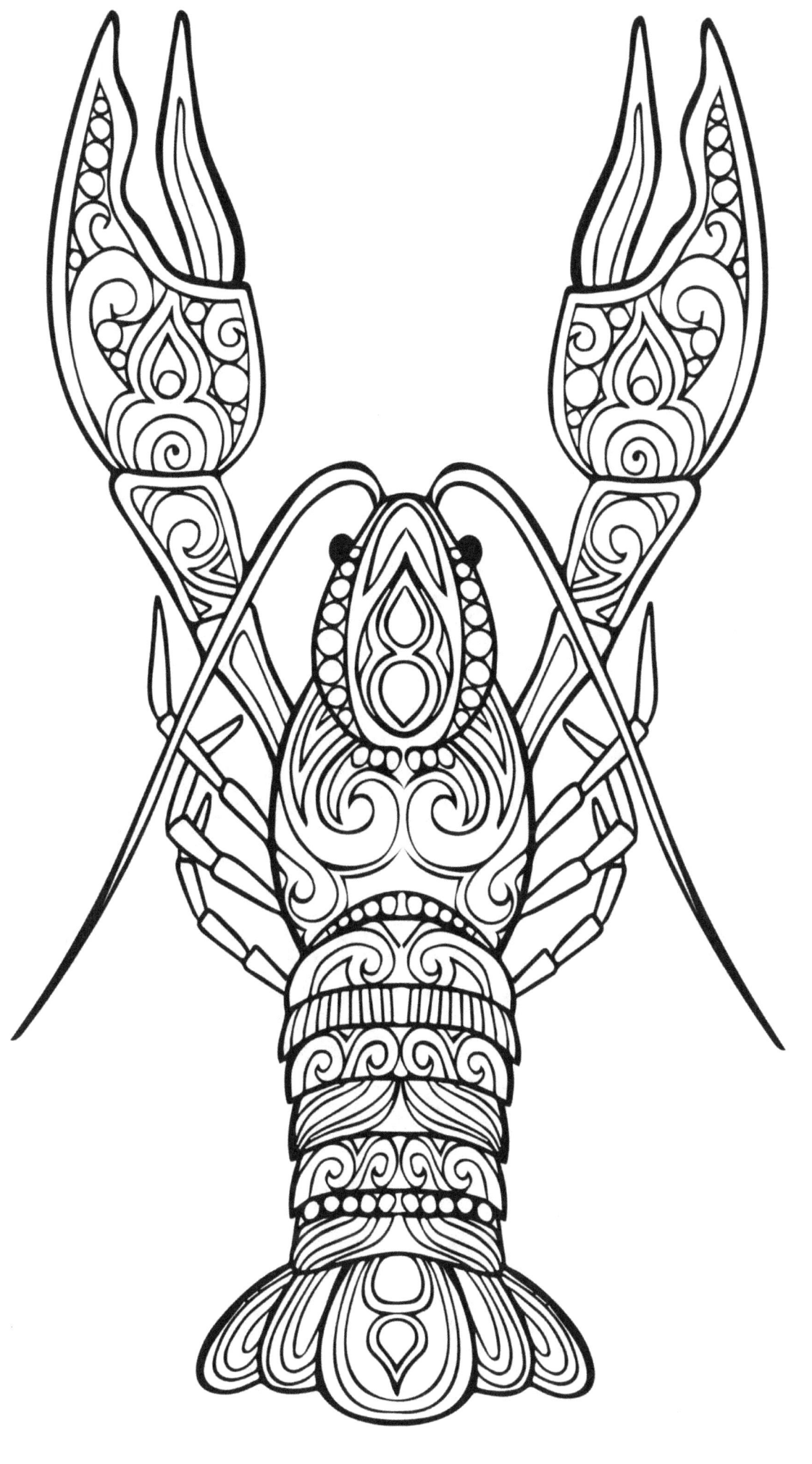

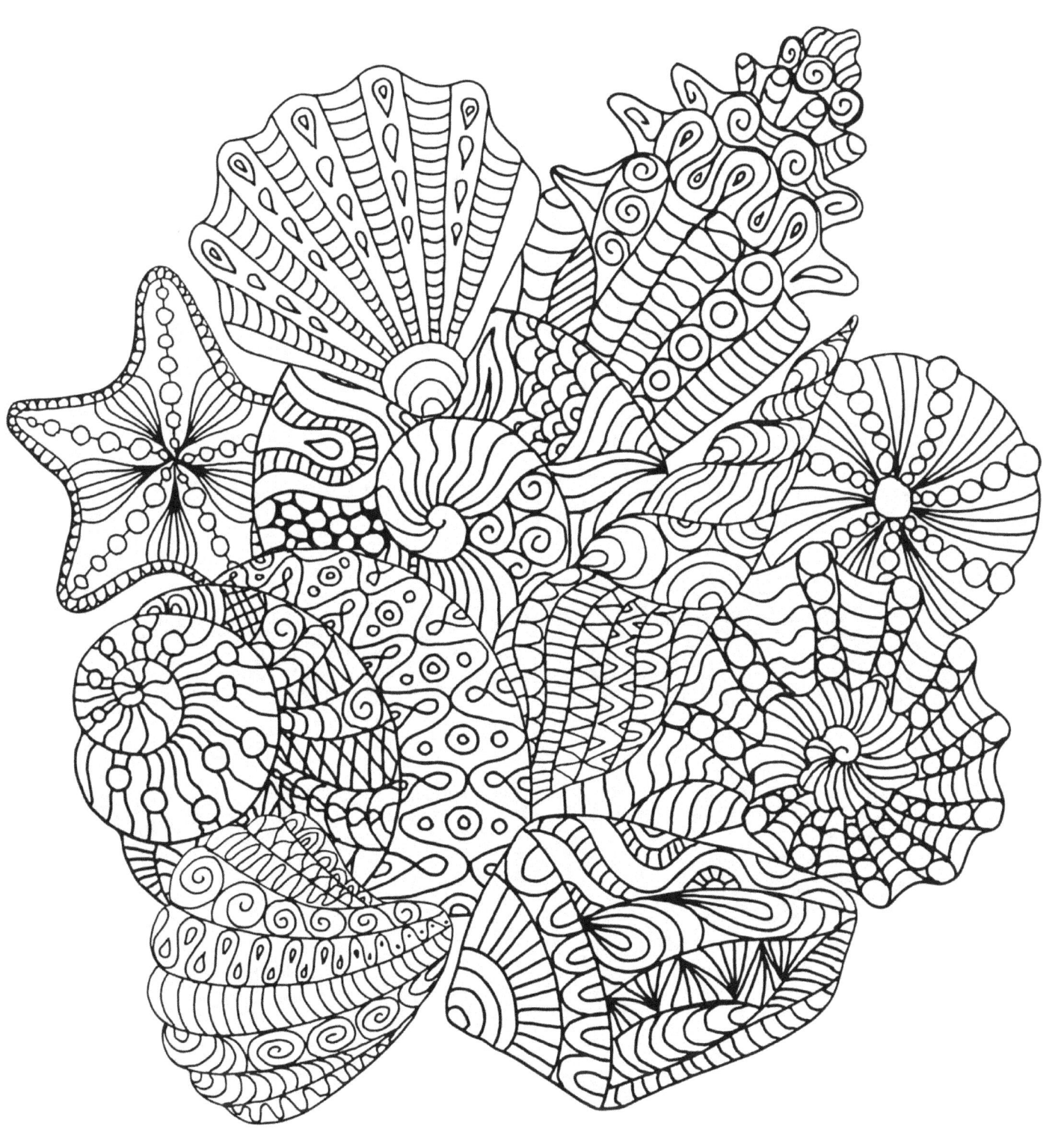

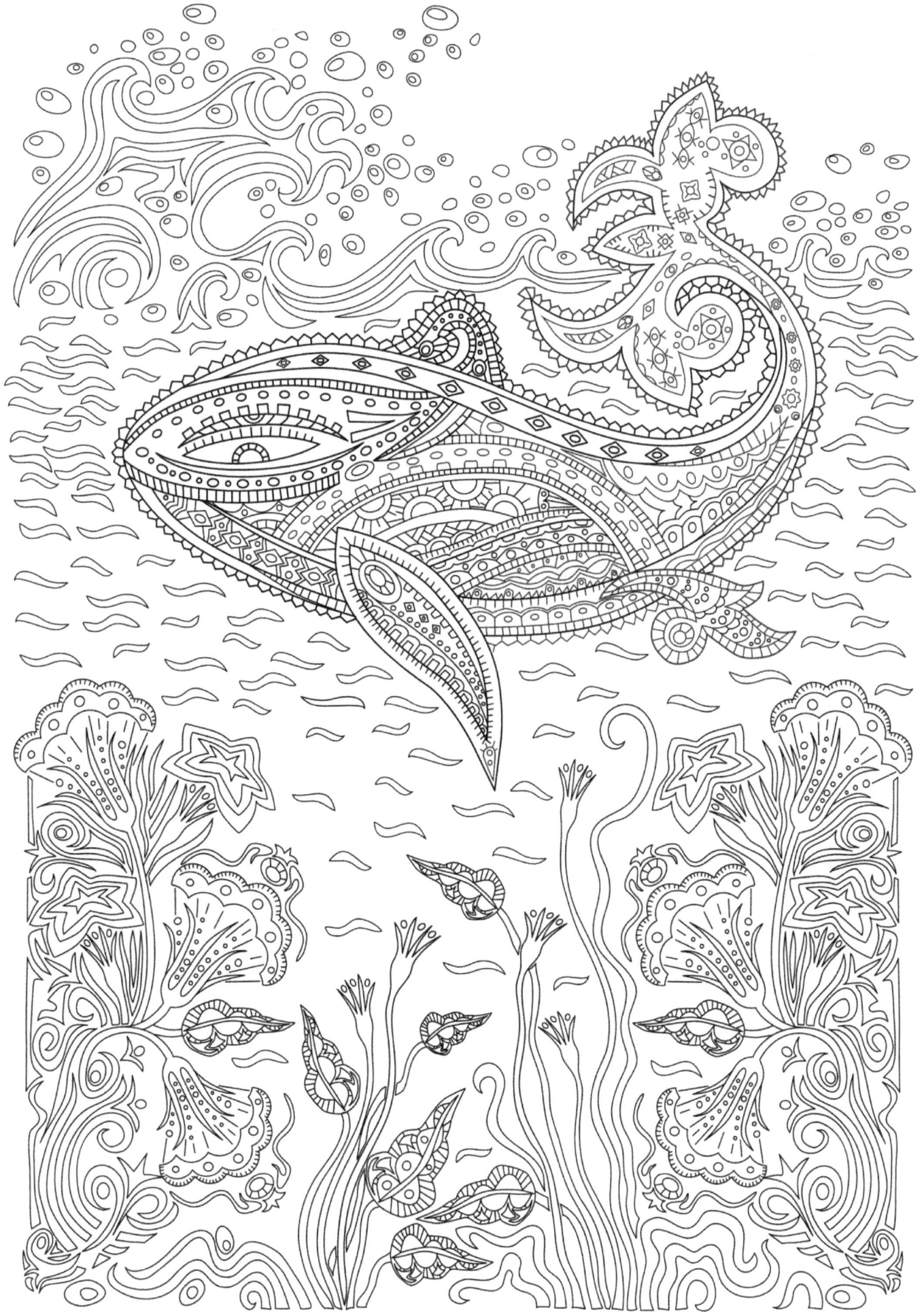

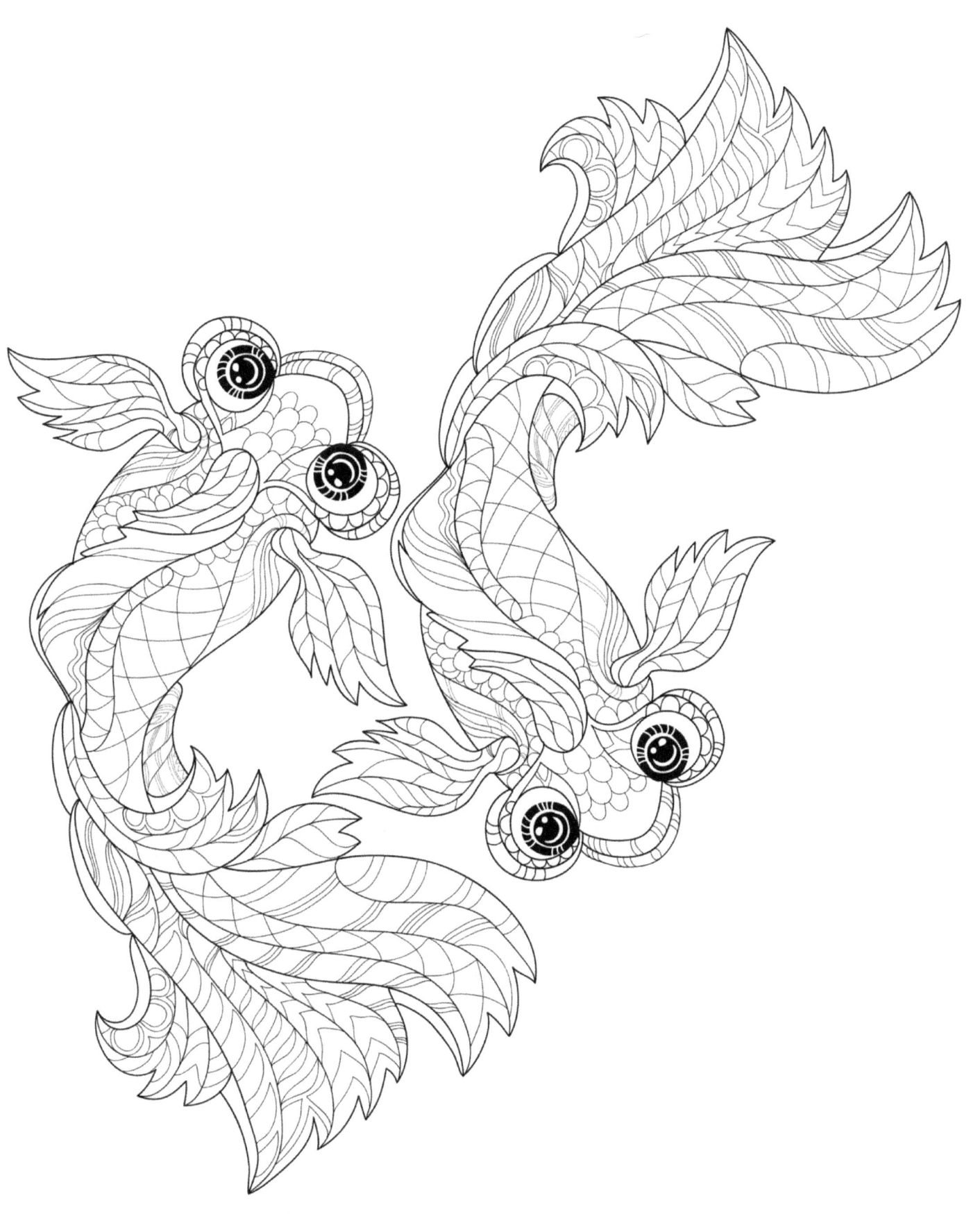

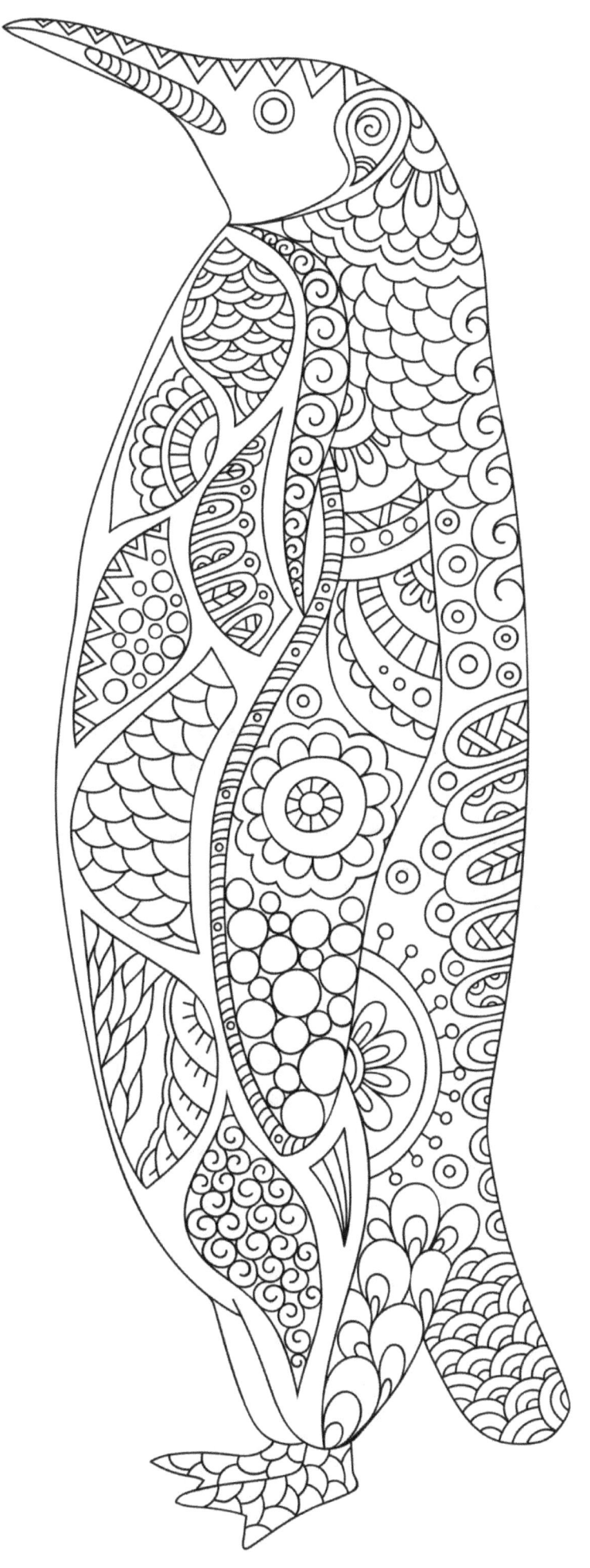

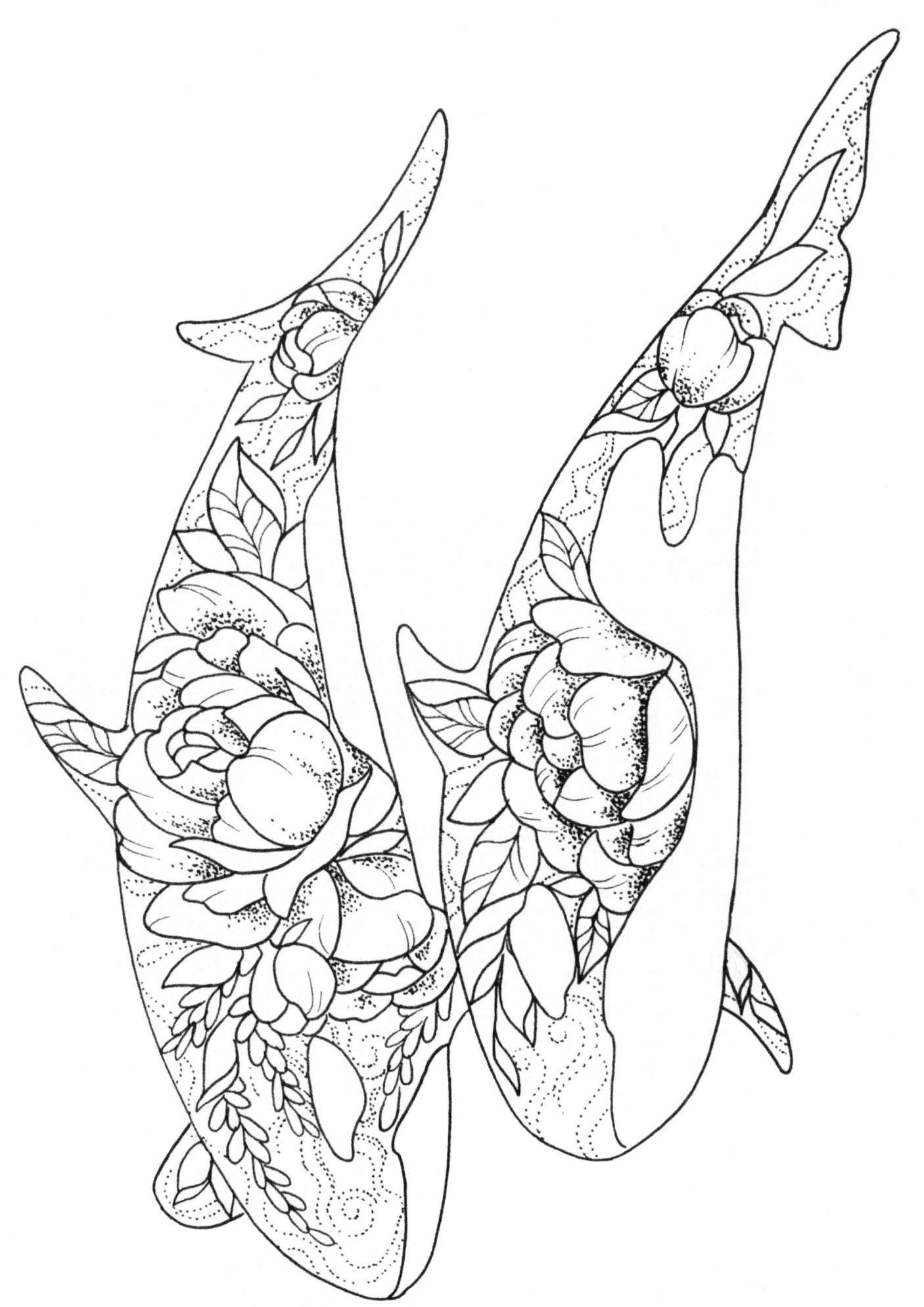

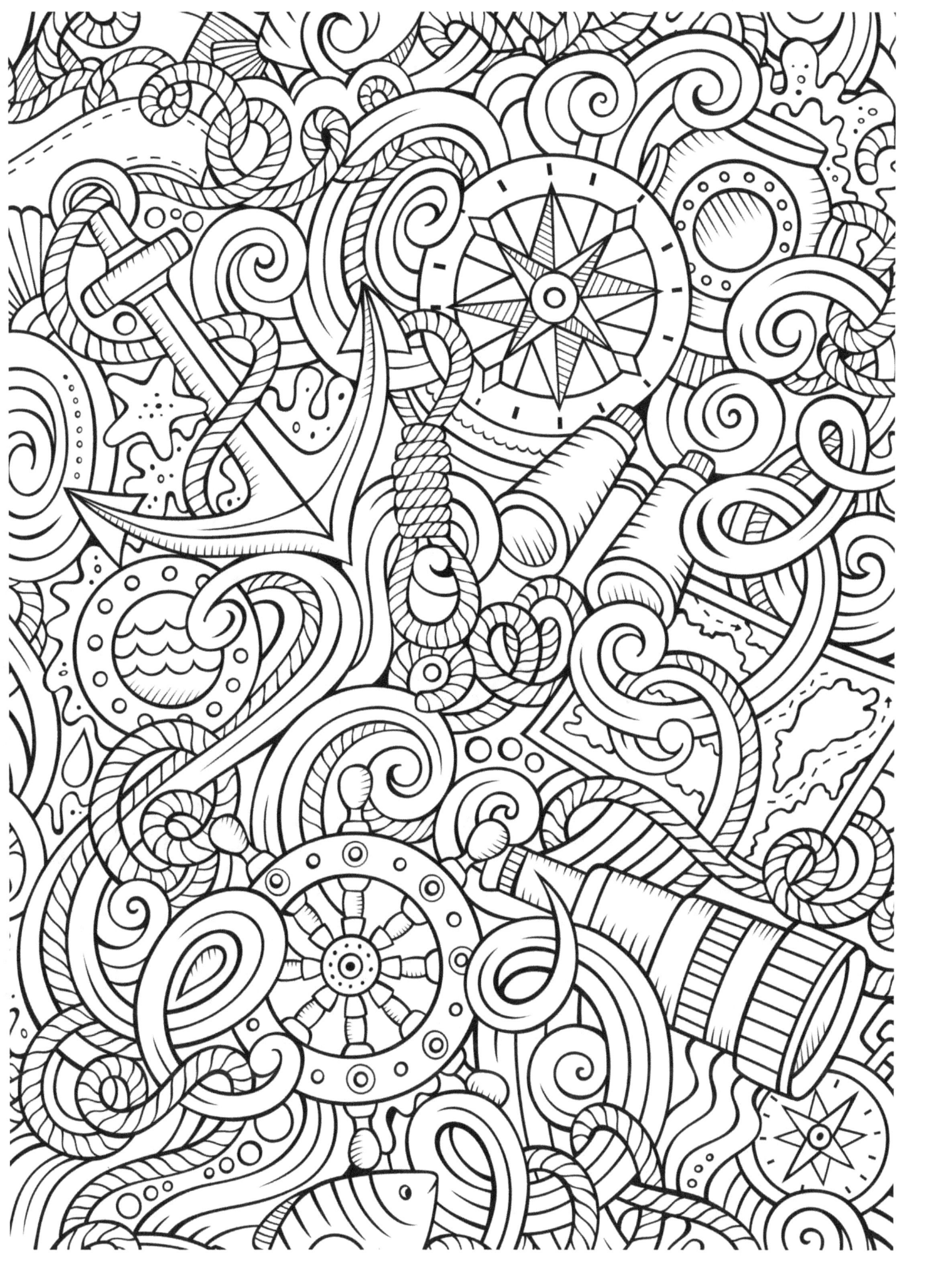

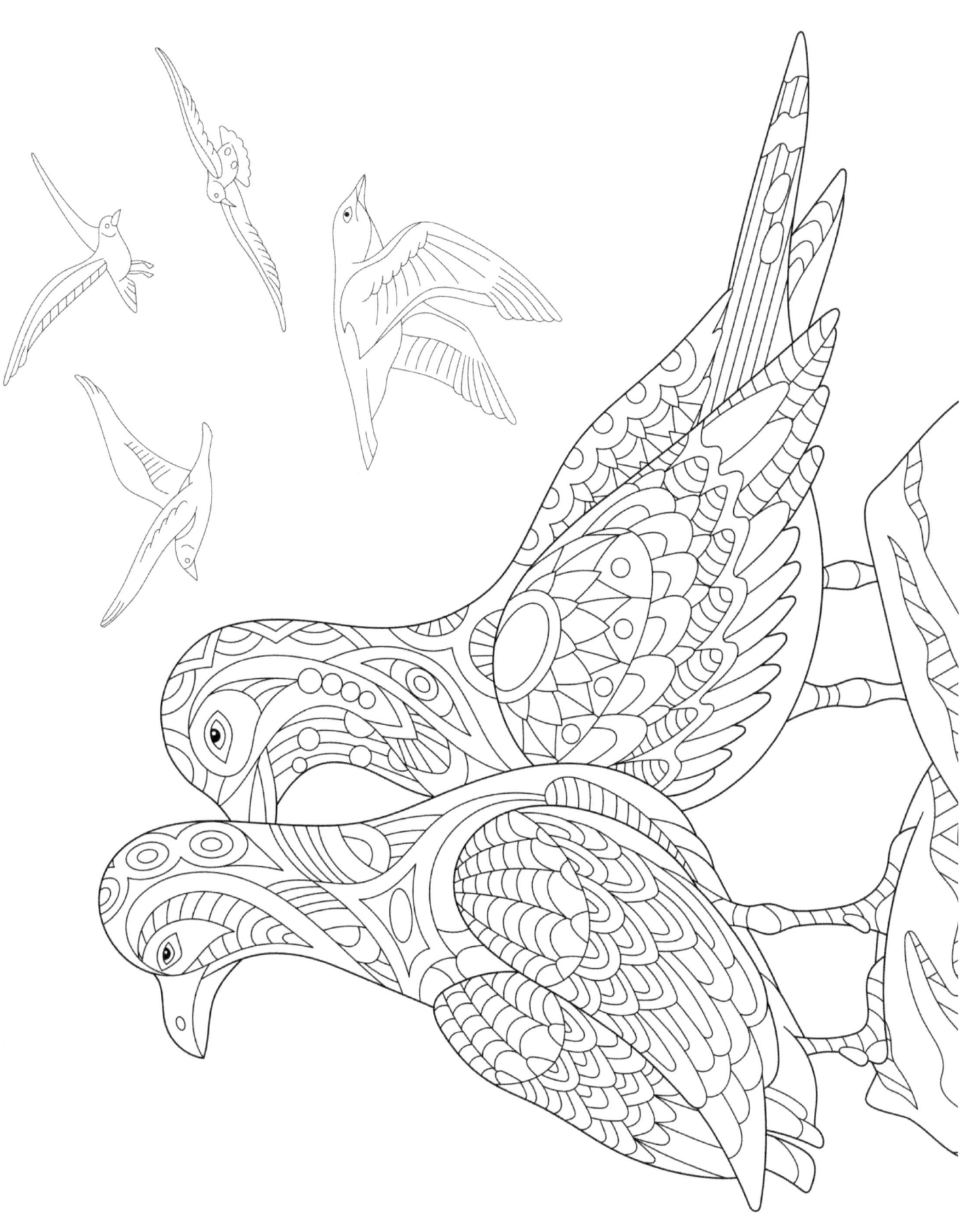

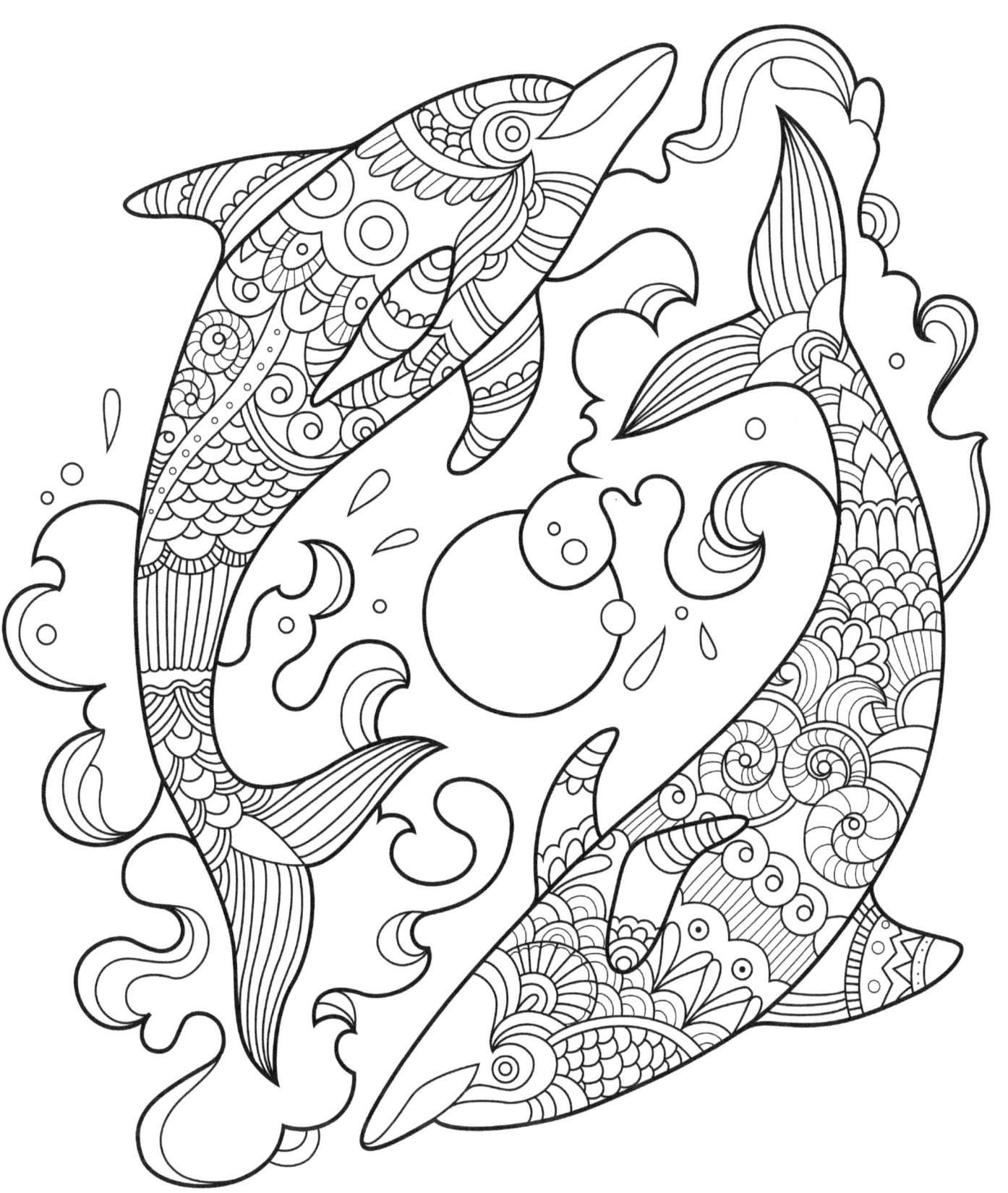

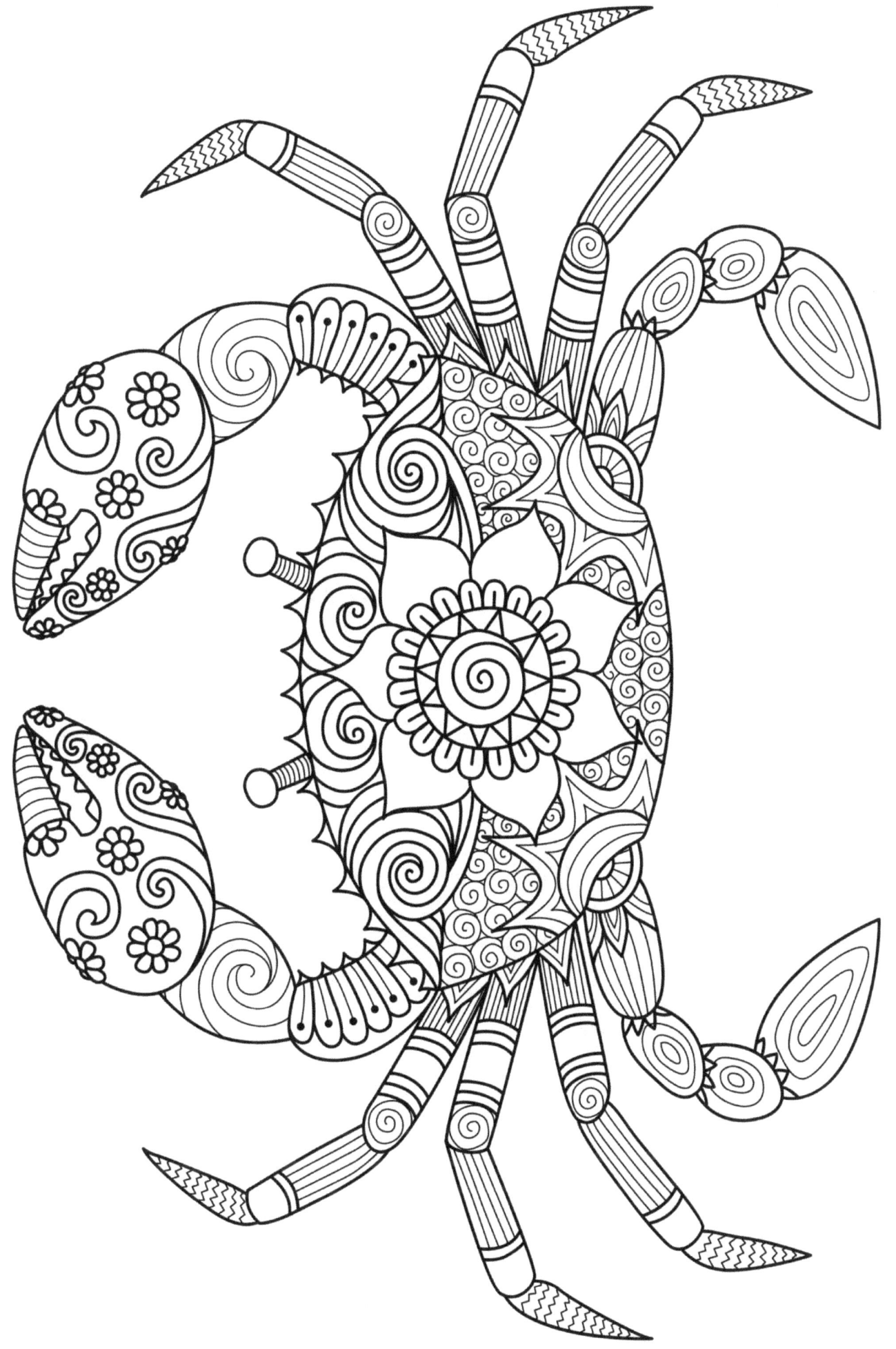